THE SPANIEL SURVIVAL GUIDE

THE SPANIEL SURVIVAL GUIDE

Jacqueline Boyd

THE CROWOOD PRESS

CONTENTS

INTRODUCTION: THE SPANIEL SURVIVAL GUIDE – YOUR ESSENTIAL GUIDE TO LIVING WITH SPANIELS

I saw the puppy instantly. A little blue roan Cocker Spaniel, front feet on the mesh of the kennel door and a tail wagging furiously. My first spaniel. The arrival of 'Megan' was a pivotal event in my world. Here I am twenty odd years later, surrounded by spaniels, writing about them. I did not start out with spaniels but with labradors and poodles. I still have soft spots for these breeds. However, spaniels and particularly cockers, have absolutely stolen my heart and 'got under my skin'.

In the years since Megan sparked my enthusiasm for spaniels, I have built a personal and professional life around animals, dogs particularly. Thanks to spaniels, I have made epic mistakes. I have been made to look an absolute fool. I have had to extricate myself from hilariously awkward situations. I have had some of the absolute best days of my life and some of the absolute worst. I have competed and demonstrated at Crufts, the world's biggest dog show. I have laughed and cried, cuddled, and cared for spaniels. I have made lifelong

Success in a gundog working test with Molly (Millsey Pinot of Clonameg AWS) and her daughter, Mini-Moo (Clonameg Miorbhail Dubh).

friends (human and canine) and had experiences that I never dreamed of. As well as all of that, I have had the companionship and love (yes, I will call it love) of some of the most wonderful canine friends that I will never forget. All of this was possible because of that little blue roan Cocker Spaniel puppy and the wonderful dog she became.

Megan gave me the spaniel bug and before I knew it, I had a multi-spaniel household – something I now understand is a not-uncommon occurrence. I currently live with six cocker spaniels, all loosely related to Megan if I go far enough back in their pedigrees (although this is pretty standard with pedigreed dogs anyway). I have lived with dogs and bitches and experienced the quirks and characters of each. I have seen puppies whelped and grow into fabulous companions, working and sporting dogs. I have rehomed spaniels and known puppies from the minute they came into the world. I have been there as they took their last breath and broke my heart, something I know will happen time and time again. I have thoroughly invested myself into spaniels, and cockers especially.

Most of all, I have learned and still am learning. This is one of the wonderful things about dogs - sharing your life with them means you have to learn and be eternally curious. Knowing what makes them tick and how to live harmoniously with dogs is essential. For spaniels in particular, their ancestry, and other characteristics, can create specific challenges that can test the patience and resilience of even the most laid-back caregiver.

This brings me to this book. I have wanted to write a book about living with spaniels for a long time. If I had spent as much time writing as I have spent talking about 'my book idea', this could have been finished years ago. Megan started this – my passion for a breed and a deep desire to make the world a better place for dogs and their people.

WHY THE SPANIEL SURVIVAL GUIDE?

The humanisation and altered role of dogs in society has resulted in a weird paradox. We know more about dogs, their behaviour, health, nutrition and overall biology than ever before. Dogs should have wonderful lives, but they don't always. Behaviour problems and concerns are increasingly common and, for many

Spaniel puppies with a fun-filled life ahead of them.

The joy of spaniels.

spaniels, caregivers struggle with self-hunting, frustration and separation related behaviours, recall issues and extreme resource possessiveness. Health issues as a result of genetic conditions or lifestyle are increasingly problematic. Meeting the intrinsic needs of spaniels and remembering their ancestry and origin is more important now than ever, thanks to their popularity and the changed expectations of dogs in society.

This book is intended for anyone who lives with or thinks they would like to live with a spaniel as a companion. This is not just a manual about the care and training of spaniels. There are many other fabulous resources available that offer more in-depth advice and guidance about the specifics of care and management, as well as the intricacies of training. Instead, this is a collection of lessons I have learned and things I wish I knew initially, with a liberal sprinkling of the various trials and tribulations that living with spaniels brings. There is also coverage of some of the most common challenges that novice spaniel caregivers experience.

One thing that cannot be underestimated though, is the absolute joy my spaniels bring into my life, and this book is very much a celebration of that. My hope is that this book deepens our appreciation and understanding of spaniels and who they are and how to use that understanding to create a mutually harmonious and happy life together.

Welcome to *The Spaniel Survival Guide* – buckle up, because like everything with spaniels, it is likely to be a little manic, might lose focus at times and be occasionally distracted, but is ultimately loyal and true. I hope that you enjoy this book, whether you are a seasoned spaniel 'carer', new to spaniels, a dog-lover or someone who appreciates the depth and value of the human-animal bond and wants to learn about the joy of 'surviving spaniels'.

CHAPTER 1

CHOOSING YOUR SPANIEL

Is a spaniel for you? Will a spaniel make a fantastic family member and companion? What should you know before considering a spaniel? And, most importantly, how do you choose your spaniel once you have decided that a spaniel is for you?

A family spaniel.

SO, YOU FANCY A SPANIEL?

Spaniels are some of the most popular dogs globally. They make wonderful companions as well as dedicated work colleagues. Characterised by pendulous ears, medium height, and a happy, congenial and active personality, it is no surprise that spaniels remain firm family favourites. Indeed, the Cocker Spaniel is often known as 'the merry Cocker'. Add to these characteristics, biddability, trainability, intelligence and an optimistic outlook, plus decades of selection for desirable working traits such as hunting and retrieving. As a result, spaniels also remain popular as working gundogs and in a number of other functional roles such as detection dogs in, for example, for law enforcement, safety (explosives detection), forensics (cadaver and arson detection), conservation detection and even to detect diseases and medical conditions in their human partners.

THE HISTORY OF SPANIELS

The word 'spaniel' is thought to originate from the old French word '*espaigneul*' meaning Spanish, as spaniels were thought to originate from Spain. Spaniels were hunting partners, bred to push (flush or 'spring') game birds out of dense plant cover to be shot, initially by arrows and then by guns. These dogs then found and retrieved the shot game back to their handlers. They were classified as being land spaniels, water spaniels or toy spaniels. Over the years, specific breeds and

Spaniels remain popular as working gundogs, often working alongside other breeds.

types developed, based on the jobs they undertook and the environment in which they were going to work. This caused changes to size, shape, colour and even subtle behavioural differences too, many of which we see in the variety of spaniel breeds and types found today.

SPANIEL BREEDS AND TYPES

Spaniels are now a diverse group of dogs, ranging in size from small breeds such as the Cavalier King Charles Spaniel and American Cocker Spaniel, to the medium-sized gundog breeds of Springer and Cocker Spaniels. The Sussex, Field, Welsh and Clumber Spaniels are less commonly seen spaniel breeds in the UK, but breed afficionados continue to promote them and demonstrate their working ability, characteristics and personalities. There are also geographical specific spaniels such as the Boykin spaniel in the USA.

The much larger and very distinctive Irish Water Spaniel has a characteristic densely curled coat and long, whiplike tail. They have long ears and retain a typical spaniel-like, fun-loving personality. However, the Irish Water Spaniel is more accurately viewed as a retriever in terms of working and training expectations.

In terms of popularity, the Cocker Spaniel and Springer Spaniel remain two of the most numerically common, registered breeds. Their congeniality, biddability, size and even societal familiarity mean they are and are likely to remain firm favourites in the dog world. The minority spaniel breeds, mixes and crosses all retain similar physical and behavioural characteristics too, albeit with their own specific breed standards, idiosyncrasies and distinctive characteristics. Your individual preferences and lifestyle situation requirements are likely to play a part in deciding if and what type of spaniel is ideal for you.

Spaniels and spaniel crosses

Spaniels are often described as 'clown-like' and often have impressive comic timing, as well as the ability to create hilarious and sometimes embarrassing situations for their people. It is strongly recommended

Spaniels are a diverse group of different breeds and types, all with the typical long, pendulous ears.

A 'sprocker' spaniel – a cross between a Springer Spaniel and a Cocker Spaniel.

that you have a sense of humour if you intend to share your life with a spaniel!

These traits can be seen across the many classic, recognised breeds of spaniels, as well as the various crosses including the common 'sprocker spaniel' (springer-cocker cross). Many spaniel characteristics will also be seen in other common crosses with labradors ('springador' or 'cockador') or collies ('sprollies'), although to a lesser extent, thanks to the genetic influence of the other breeds.

Spaniels are sensitive souls

Spaniels are sensitive souls and do not take well to harsh or punitive handling. Because spaniels can appear outwardly very 'busy', this can often disguise their sensitive side. A spaniel that suddenly starts 'the zoomies' – frantic running in circles – is most probably indicating that they are conflicted in how best to respond to a given situation. They are not being 'bad' or 'disobedient'. They can also worry about situations that might have scared them or made them feel uncomfortable. This is why fair, empathetic training and positive associations with the world are so important to support your spaniel throughout life and the sooner you can build a relationship on these grounds with your puppy, the better.

Show-line spaniels versus working-line spaniels

An important distinction to be aware of – especially with Cockers and Springers – is the difference between 'show bred' dogs and 'working-bred' dogs. For some of the minority spaniel breeds such as the Sussex, Field and Clumber, the distinction between

Early training and positive world experiences are essential for your spaniel puppy.

working and show lines is less pronounced, although some breeders select and breed specifically for the show ring or working ability.

In the case of pedigree Springers and Cockers in the UK, they are registered simply as 'Spaniel (springer)' or 'Spaniel (cocker)' without distinction of whether they are originally from showing lines or working lines. This can be confusing to new spaniel caregivers – how do you know if a dog comes from show lines or working lines, and what should you expect? This can be important because some working line spaniels are the canine version of a Formula 1 car – wonderful dogs but potentially not the best choice for a sedate and spaniel-inexperienced family home.

Firstly, if you are looking for a puppy, a responsible breeder will advise you clearly on the origin of your puppy, their ancestry and what this means for their temperament and personality. Looking at pedigrees can also be helpful. Many kennel names will be associated with specific activities and sporting disciplines, and you can quickly become familiar with the show kennel names and the working kennel names. If you are absolutely new to spaniels, it is strongly recommended to seek advice from other spaniel caregivers about breeders or other organisations that might be supportive in your search.

A kennel name, also known as an 'affix', is a consistent name or word that appears in the registered names of all dogs from a specific kennel/registered owner(s). A kennel name needs to be registered with the relevant country of residence's kennel club/ registration organisation before use but can then be added to the name of dogs owned or bred by that kennel and caregiver who holds the affix. Where the kennel name appears at the start of a registered name (the prefix), it indicates the dog was bred by that kennel. If it appears at the end of a registered name (the suffix), then the dog was bred and brought in from elsewhere.

Other ways to get a feel for the origin and ancestry of your spaniel is to look for other indications of purpose or competitive success on any registered names. This will typically be seen as letters added

Megan – my first cocker who gave rise to my affix 'Clonameg' – a portmanteau of 'clone a Megan'.

Millsey Pinot of Clonameg AWS. The AWS signifies that she achieved her silver agility warrant award.

to the start or end of a dog's registered (rather than their pet/call) name. If you see registered names in the pedigree with ShCh as a prefix, this indicates the dog is a show champion and has excelled in the show ring. FTCh, FTAW or FTW indicate that the dog has excelled in field trials, as a field trial champion, field trial award winner or field trial winner, although FTCh is the only official title that is utilised – others tend to be used to indicate a dog's success and for awareness by others. There are other titles and awards that will also be seen adjacent to registered names, and these will indicate achievement and success in a range of other activities.

Spaniels from showing lines have heavier coats, more feathering on their legs and undercarriage and are more aligned with the typical physical and colour 'breed standard' expectations than working bred spaniels. Show bred dogs may be slightly less naturally 'driven' than working-line dogs, meaning they might naturally be less active, but not always.

Dogs bred with 'lots of red' in the pedigree means there are many ancestors who have excelled and been titled. This can be a sign of thoughtful breeding and careful selection. It may also indicate that working-line dogs bred in this way are highly driven and likely to need significant physical and mental stimulation. Be prepared to meet those needs in such spaniels, otherwise life can be miserable for you both.

However, there is as much potential for variation within these groups as there is between them. There is no guarantee that a working-bred spaniel will be more energetic than a show-bred spaniel. It is quite possible for show-bred dogs to work well and be successful in sporting activities. However, it is unlikely that working-bred dogs would meet the show breed standard or be successful in the show ring.

IS A SPANIEL RIGHT FOR YOU?

Your ambitions and intent may determine your choice of spaniel – if you aspire to grace the show ring, then looking for show-bred lines is a very sensible place to start. Breeders will also be able to advise on how to get started with ring craft and the nuances of show ring etiquette.

If your ambitions are less show ring and more activity based (active pet, working gundog, agility, canicross) then a working-line spaniel might be a good fit. For companionship, either show- or working-bred will fit the bill and your decision might come down to the time to be spent caring for your spaniel's coat and how active your everyday lifestyle is or is not.

Whatever you do choose, when you bring a spaniel into your life, be prepared for a happy, fun-loving companion who will become an integral part of your life and lifestyle, providing you with joy, laughter and delightful companionship.

If you really want to know if a spaniel is for you, consider if you are happy to regularly venture outside in all weathers to join them for exercise – they are active dogs after all! Even the smaller spaniel breeds enjoy exercise, so do not think they will be sofa dogs only.

Consider your time availability and desire to care for their coat, especially those ears that can be prone to developing mats and dreadlocks overnight. Spaniels often 'acquire' vegetation, twigs and other plant material during their expeditions, as well as enjoying mud and water – can you cope? While regular grooming is an essential part of all canine management, a thick, heavy coat does need daily attention and care, so needs to be factored into your time budget.

Spaniels are also loyal companions and actively enjoy the company of their people, often over the company of other dogs. They can become 'little shadows', determined to be in your presence whenever possible. I was once told that spaniels would get under your skin if they could – this is certainly something I have experienced with mine. Even reticent spaniels will occasionally choose to spend time in close proximity to you. This can be endearing or annoying, depending on your perspective, so is definitely something to be aware of. It can also lead to potential concerns about separation-related behaviours, so careful management and supportive training can help you and your spaniel live in harmony together.

Spaniels often become little shadows and will typically choose to spend lots of time in very close proximity, if given the chance.

FINDING YOUR SPANIEL FRIEND

You might already have everything planned and know exactly who is coming to live with you and when. Alternatively, you might be just starting to consider how best to find your new spaniel friend and what you should look for.

There are different options open to you. You might want to experience puppyhood. You might already know that you really dislike the puppy stages and would prefer to rehome an older spaniel, either through personal connections or via a rehoming organisation or charity. Each have pros and cons, and it is important to consider what will work best for you AND your new companion.

Spaniels make for fabulous canine counterparts.

Puppyhood can be an absolute joy or something to be endured, depending on your perspective!

Getting a puppy

For many people, a puppy is the first option considered. You get the joy (and occasional stress and worry!) of seeing a puppy grow and develop. If you have ambitions to train for specific activities, you can start building training foundations from the first day that puppy comes home. Some people absolutely adore the puppy stage and relish the time spent caring and training. For others, the puppy stage is something to be endured until a more mature dog 'emerges' a few months later.

Finding a breeder

Finding a breeder of a suitable puppy is the first step. While many puppies are advertised, do plan ahead – sometimes months and years – to get a puppy from a breeder that aligns with your desires and also to get a puppy that meets your needs. A good breeder will make sure that you can meet the puppy's needs too! Many new canine caregivers spend more time researching their next car than a puppy who will be an integral part of their lives for at least a decade. Time spent planning and researching your puppy is absolutely time well spent.

There are commercial breeders with several breeds of dogs and produce multiple litters per year. There are also hobby breeders who rarely breed, usually have a single breed of dog, and will only produce a litter when they wish to keep their breeding lines going. You might also come across people who have simply decided that they want their bitch to have a litter. Occasionally, puppies end up with rehoming organisations too, so it can be worth being registered with these if you would like a puppy to join your household.

There are pros and cons to where you source your puppy. It is useful to speak to people with spaniels of the breed and type that you like, asking them where their spaniel is from. This can be a great way of making connections with breeders that might not otherwise be possible – many small breeders never advertise. Be aware of local regulations regarding dog breeding and animal welfare too – there are limitations and commercial, high-volume breeders need to be compliant.

YOUR PUPPY SEARCH

There are plenty of things to bear carefully in mind when you begin searching for your perfect puppy, both positive and negative:

RED FLAGS TO WATCH OUT FOR IN YOUR PUPPY SEARCH:

- A breeder who has multiple breeds and produces many litters per year (these can look very slick in terms of marketing and have impressive facilities, so be aware).
- Not being able to meet the mum of the puppies and learn about their relatives.
- Instant availability of puppies or puppies in unusual, 'rare' colours – merle is not a standard colour for most spaniel breeds, for example.
- No questioning of you about your ability to provide an ideal home for the puppy.
- Not allowing you to visit the puppy or see the facility and where the puppies are raised.
- No health tests being undertaken on the puppy's parents – if health tests have been done, the results should be freely available.
- Not allowing you any choice in puppy selection (although sometimes with small litters, other puppies will already have been reserved and sometimes breeders are better placed at knowing the personality of puppies and thus, their suitability for certain homes).
- Puppies being reared in an environment that is barren and lacking in stimulation and learning opportunities.
- Very high prices – breeding is not cheap, but excessively high costs are more about making money than supporting the progression, health and welfare of a breed.
- No information about pedigrees, registration documents, veterinary health checks, de-worming, microchipping, or other essential information.
- Permitting rehoming of puppies at less than eight weeks of age (this is illegal in the UK).
- No follow-up advice, guidance or lifetime support, including a contract/agreement that details the responsibilities of the breeder and the new caregiver.

Puppies should be raised in clean and stimulating environments.

If at any point in your puppy search you feel uncomfortable, walk away. This even applies if you feel that you need to 'rescue' a puppy from a less-than-ideal situation. Every year, new caregivers are distraught when their new puppy falls ill or turns out to have a health or behavioural condition and the breeder can no longer be contacted. If you do end up in such a situation, report the facility to local animal welfare and trading standards organisations.

GREEN FLAGS TO LOOK FOR IN YOUR PUPPY SEARCH:

- A breeder who interviews you at length, long before you actually get to meet their dogs or the puppies.
- A breeder who has their older, retired dogs still living as part of the family.
- They might have multiple dogs, even of a couple of breeds, but the dogs are part of the family and not permanently in kennels or outside buildings.
- A waiting list that does not necessarily ask for a deposit and allows you to change your mind – a good breeder will always want the best for their puppies and their new people, especially if circumstances change.
- Health tests (with results freely available) and evidence of competitive/training success to support breeding choices; even evidence of producing well-rounded companion dogs is important – not all breeders will be training or competing to a high level and instead just enjoy their breed.
- Being able to meet the parents (note that often the stud dog lives elsewhere, but their information should be available) and visit the puppies (perhaps even via social media) before they come home – some breeders will limit access to very young puppies because of potential disease transmission risk.
- Puppies being supplied with a 'puppy pack' of essential equipment (usually a couple of weeks' worth of the puppy food being used, essential documentation, some familiar bedding, toys and other useful items).
- A breeder who has undertaken early training and socialisation with the puppies – car trips, crate training, toilet training, basic recall and lead walking, wearing a collar and so on.
- A breeder who advises you and supports you on the puppy best suited for you, as well as a breeder who might say 'I am really sorry, but I do not feel these puppies are ideally suited for you at the moment.'
- A clear 'contract' and information about support, advice and guidance – many small-scale breeders will retain close connections with ALL their puppies and a breeder who states that a puppy (even as an adult) should be returned to them should the new caregiver's situation change has a clear interest in the future of that puppy.

I always remember being grilled at length, interview-like, by the breeder of my first Cocker Spaniel, before I actually got to meet her. It was actually quite scary on reflection, but it was clear that he wanted to make sure we could provide a good home for her and that 'puppy fever' would not hijack our competent thought processes!

QUESTIONS TO ASK A POTENTIAL BREEDER

- Why did you breed this litter and choose the sire and dam – what are their personalities like and are there any health concerns (for example, digestive issues, allergies, skin irritation) that might be relevant?
- What health tests have the parents had and can I see the results/certificates?
- Are the puppies registered with the appropriate registration body? If not, why not?
- What veterinary attention and checks have the puppies had and when? Can you have the notes?
- What has been the vaccination and deworming schedule of the dam and the puppies?
- How old is mum, how many litters has she had and how are the other puppies doing?
- Can you contact other prospective puppy people and chat to people with older puppies?
- How often can you visit the puppies?
- Where have the puppies been born and raised and what have they been exposed to?
- What toilet training has been done and what cue words have been used for specific behaviours?
- What food has been fed, how much and how many meals per day?

You should feel comfortable and confident with your puppy's breeder – they often become life-long friends and can be amazing mentors and sources of support and advice. I consider myself incredibly lucky that I remain good friends with the breeders of several of my spaniels, including the breeders of the dam of my very first spaniel who was born over twenty years ago. Similarly, I remain in contact with my own puppy people and get to regularly see many of the puppies I have bred, or my boys have sired – some of whom are now overseas.

Good breeders expose their puppies to lots of beneficial experiences before they leave.

Look for stud dog success in canine disciplines as an indication of what their puppies might be like – this is a father and son, both placed in the same agility class.

If you are interested in specific canine activities, look for the registered names of successful and competing dogs as a way of identifying their breeding. This can help you identify specific lines that you can explore intended breeding plans for, or to identify stud dogs who are producing offspring with the attributes that you like.

Choosing your puppy

You might have an idea of what you want your spaniel to be and to look like. However, often a puppy (or adult dog) will pick you! When viewing puppies, it can be really difficult to make decisions before they are about five weeks old because full personalities are still developing. Watch the litter and look for how they interact with each other, their dam, any other dogs that are in the vicinity and also people. Look for a puppy who is not overly shy, nor extremely independent (although these characteristics can change and develop, and for some people and intended purposes, are desirable!).

Ask lots of questions about your puppy. Your breeder should be happy to help.

Puppies should be relaxed and comfortable to be handled and should be clean with bright, clear eyes, no excessive discharge, no wheezing, snuffling, or coughing, no scratching or evidence of scurfiness. Bottoms should be clean as should the environment they are living in.

Breeders will be aware of any potential concerns and make you aware of them, especially if you have ambitions to breed. Hernias, for example, are relatively common and vary in severity, so should be highlighted if apparent so that you can make an informed choice. Similarly, boys should have two descended testicles, but sometimes these have not fully descended by eight weeks old, so need monitoring. Retained testicles need removing as the dog matures because of potential health issues and also precludes the dog from future breeding plans. Even aspects of your spaniel's markings and conformation (such as their dental alignment) might be relevant, especially if you aim to grace the show ring, and your breeder will be able to support you in identifying what best suits.

Pick a puppy who is healthy and alert.

A good breeder will help identify a puppy with a personality to suit you.

Your choice of puppy depends on many factors, so the more prepared you are and the more consideration you have given to how you want your spaniel to be, the more likely it is that you will have a fabulous friend.

BRINGING HOME PUPPY

Once you have sourced and planned for your new puppy to join your household, some preparation is essential before they come home. Your house and garden need to be puppy proof. Escape routes from a garden need to be secured – you might even want to use a smaller puppy pen initially to limit their exploration of the garden. Items that can be chewed or accidentally damaged by a boisterous and chewing puppy should be put out of reach. This includes potentially harmful things such as electric cables, medication, alcohol, some human foods – raisins, sultanas and chocolate especially.

You might want to use a puppy crate/pen to aid toilet training and if your puppy is already used to this from their breeder, it can become a valuable place for them to relax and settle in. It is also useful to keep them safe, especially when unsupervised – remember, your puppy is always learning, whether supervised or not. If you can limit and manage their experiences, that goes a long way to them learning good, acceptable behaviours, rather than the ones you definitely do not want.

A houseline is a long (about two metres/six feet in length) lightweight lead that you can attach to your dog's collar and leave trailing. This is useful for managing what your puppy is doing and engaging with, while also allowing some freedom. This also lays the groundwork for using a long line outdoors when training recall and encouraging your puppy to stay close to you.

Ideally, the more you can mimic what your puppy has had when with their breeder, the easier the transition to their new home will be. This might be in terms of mealtimes, rest times, bedtime and so on.

Toilet training

Hopefully, your puppy will have some great toilet training foundations already, but do not rely on them being able to immediately transfer those skills to a new home and location. Always start by taking your puppy

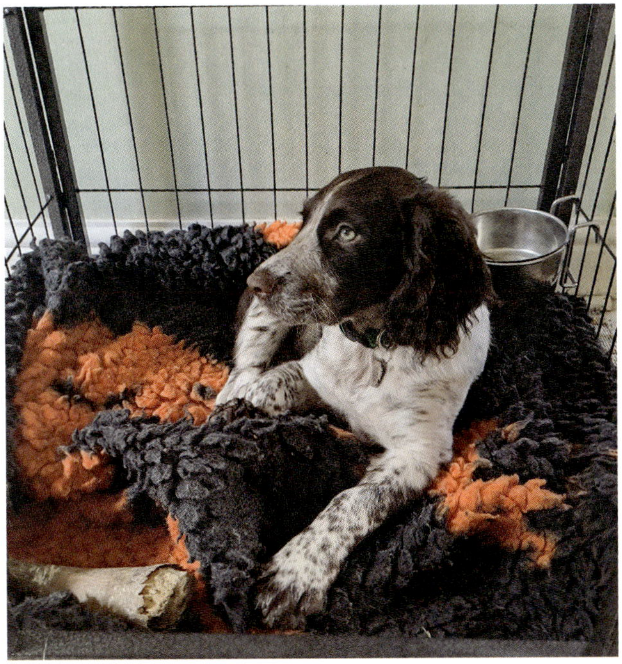

A crate or puppy pen can help to keep your puppy safe when unsupervised and also aids toilet training.

out to a desired toilet area and waiting until they 'go'. Using a cue word for toileting is useful. I say 'busy, busy' to indicate I would like them to urinate or defecate. Using a lead or a long line can also stop them getting distracted and 'forgetting' to go. Repeat multiple times a day and always after waking, eating, playing. The more you practise, the better they will be at developing the ability to hold their bladder and bowels. Always remember that as bladder control develops, puppies sometimes do not fully empty their bladder on their first 'go'. For this reason, it is good to wait and see if they realise there is some left! This prevents the annoyance of the puppy going outside, coming back inside and then having a little piddle on the carpet.

Overnight, ensure they have toileted last thing at night and if necessary, for the first few days/weeks, set your alarm during the night to get up, take them out and pop them back to bed. Time spent at this stage will pay dividends with toilet training.

Do not get complacent too fast either – just because a door is open, never assume your puppy will choose to go outside when they are small. Until a puppy is around nine months old, keep a solid toileting routine and support them in getting it right. Also be aware that any changes in the household (visitors, events, etc.), hormonal changes (for dogs and bitches), illness and even changes in seasons (darkness and poor weather can put many spaniels off going outside) can cause a regression in toileting. If your puppy does have an accident, avoid scolding them or getting angry. Quietly and calmly remove them from the area and clean it up using suitable cleaners to remove the smells that can sometimes make going in the same place again more likely.

Some breeders will use puppy pads for toilet training. I have always found simply taking the puppy outside for toileting has been easier and resulted in faster and more robust appropriate toilet behaviours, but you can decide what is most suitable for your own individual situations. I have also had success using artificial grass toilet mats in puppy pens to encourage puppies to toilet in a set area. Those mats can then be taken outside to create a specific toilet area that is familiar to the puppy. Using a pen or a crate can also be useful as dogs will generally avoid toileting in their sleeping area, but you must let your puppy out regularly and use the crate or pen for supportive management, not as a punishment or for prolonged periods of time.

The first night for puppy

Ideally, your puppy's breeder will have given them a great start in life and prepared them for their new home. This might have involved separating them from their mum and siblings for increasing periods of time in the days before being collected. However, for any puppy, the transition to a new home, new people and other dogs/animals, new environment – sometimes with a long car journey in between – can be distressing. The first night for many puppies can be a lonely and scary experience, but equally for others, they adapt really well and settle quickly.

It is worth knowing where you want your puppy to sleep for the first few nights and, if they are upset, crying, whining or barking, gently comfort them. Make sure they are warm, have a full tummy and do not need the toilet. Offer them companionship, perhaps sleeping beside them or being very close to them. Cuddly toys also mimic their litter mates. Leaving them to 'cry it out' is not fair or effective and can lead to further problems and impact on your relationship with your puppy, not to mention your ability to sleep. As with toilet training, time spent at this stage can help your puppy learn that they are safe and cared for and reduce the risks of separation-related behaviours escalating.

On the first night, start planning your expectations of your puppy, including with other household members too. This might mean deciding whether the puppy is allowed on furniture or upstairs – remember not to let them jump on and off furniture or go up and down stairs until they are physically mature, to protect their developing joints. Cue words for specific behaviours and skills should also be identified for consistency – a list of these pinned somewhere for all to see, and to add to, is a great idea so that all household members know what to expect from your new puppy.

Puppy teething and biting

One of the most common complaints of new spaniel puppy caregivers is the puppy biting. Those little puppy teeth are like needles – sharp and unrelenting. They can cause quite significant damage to skin, clothing and any items that end up in their mouths. It is definitely something that seems to vary in intensity and persistence. I have had puppies that barely did it at all and others who were scarily intense in how hard and frequently they would indulge in this behaviour.

It is an entirely natural thing for puppies to do – as natural as peeing and pooping. Puppies explore the world, at least in part, via their mouth and are learning about how 'things' react – whether that is their

Make sure your puppy's bed is safe and welcoming.

Examples of Some Cue Words

Cue Word	Expectations/Behaviour	Notes
'name'	Eye contact to be made and to be ready for follow-on cue.	Single, short whistle peep.
Come	Return to close proximity.	Multiple whistle peeps.
Wait	Hold your position until a follow-on cue is given.	
Stay	Hold your position until I return and release you.	
Free	Release cue – from a stay/other position or when lead is removed.	
Heel	Walk at my left-hand side with your shoulder level with my knee.	
Side	Walk at my right-hand side with your shoulder level with my knee.	
Sit	Sit on your haunches until another cue is given (or released).	Long single whistle peep.
Down	Lie down in sphinx position until another cue is given (or released).	
Stand	Stand squarely until another cue is given (or released).	
'Busy'	Go toilet (urinate but also to encourage defecation too).	
Bed	Go to your bed.	

mum, their siblings, objects and us. The challenge for us is to help them learn what is acceptable and teeth on human skin – not acceptable at all.

It is a behaviour that is often worse where there is not a tolerant older resident dog or dogs. When a puppy grabs another dog with their teeth, the other dog will usually gently 'correct' and sometimes reprimand the puppy. This is important for the puppy to learn appropriate social skills and also 'bite inhibition' – that is how much pressure is acceptable when interacting with others. If there is not another dog, we have to help them learn – but not by behaving as another dog would.

Puppy biting is often worst from about four to sixteen weeks old. From about sixteen weeks of age, adult teeth will be coming through and those needle-like puppy teeth starting to fall out. During teething, offer lots of appropriate chews and toys to soothe your puppy and encourage them to chew on suitable objects and not your furniture. Frozen carrots are often good options and ice cubes are sometimes enjoyed too.

When there is puppy biting, it is often linked to being tired, excited, stressed or otherwise aroused (because of excitement or anxiety). This means that being aware of how your puppy is feeling is a good start and then managing their environment to reduce the risk of biting escalating.

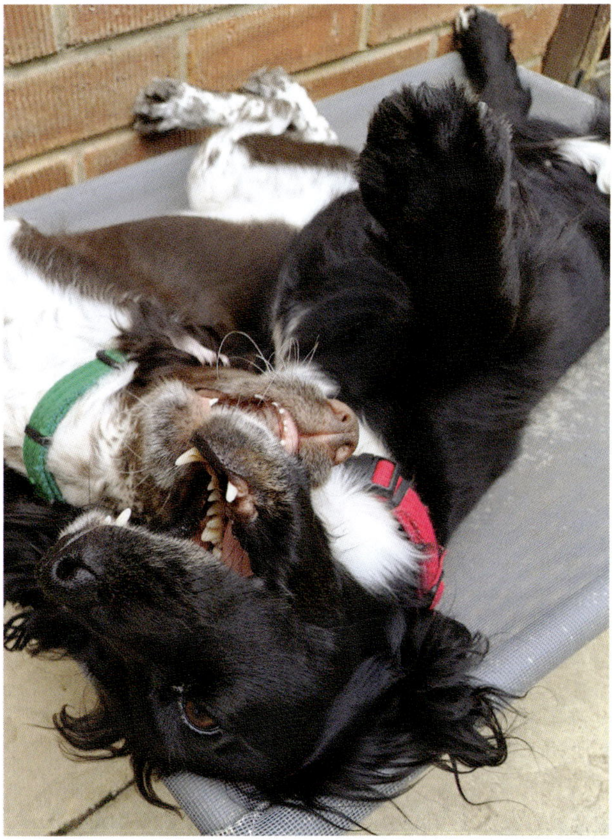

Puppy biting and mouthing is a natural behaviour, but one that does need management.

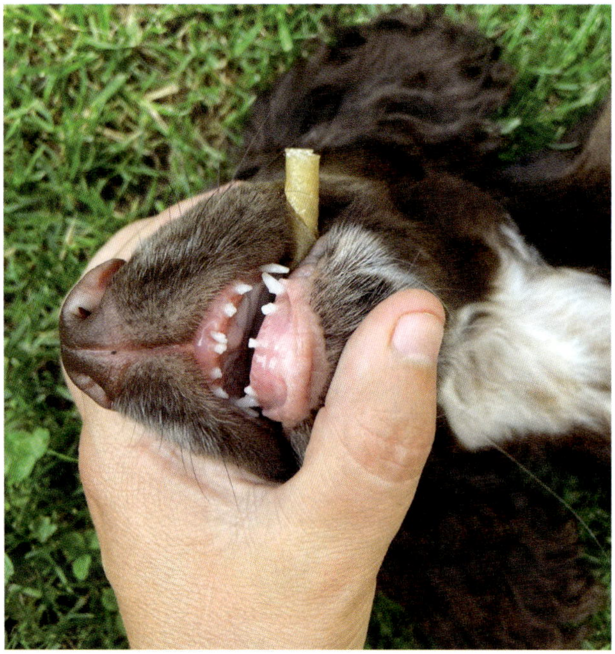

Encourage your teething puppy to chew on suitable toys and chew items.

Rehoming an adolescent or adult spaniel

While a new puppy is exciting and super cute, you might prefer to rehome an older spaniel. Sadly, lots of dogs, through no fault of their own, end up in a rescue or rehoming situation and given the chance, make the most wonderful companions. There are specific organisations and charities that specialise in spaniels, including breed-specific rescue organisations, so it is worth keeping in touch with these to find your new companion.

Sometimes older spaniels have health or behavioural concerns (minor or more significant), so it is worth making sure you are fully aware of what to expect and why the rehoming is needed. Many working-line spaniels unfortunately end up needing to be rehomed as they hit eight months old, and their caregivers realise that they are unable to offer what their dog needs in terms of activity and stimulation. Others show signs of resource possessiveness or separation-related behaviours. A reputable rehoming organisation will ensure you are fully aware of this and offer support and guidance.

THINGS THAT YOU CAN DO TO MANAGE PUPPY BITING

- Keep a routine of rest and play – this can help your puppy learn to regulate themselves and puppies do need to sleep for most of the day.
- Offer and hold chew items for them – this helps to build your connection with them as well as teaching them they can chew in your vicinity, just not on you!
- Have and manage 'little and often' interactions with your puppy (and also watch interactions with others); if the interaction is starting to 'boil over', respond and steady the behaviour and interaction. Physically remove the puppy if necessary.
- Teach a conditioned disengage cue that is paired with an alternative but incompatible behaviour – for example say 'ouchy' when teeth touch skin and do a food scatter or present a tuggy toy – note that the word is said calmly and quietly so as not to over-arouse the situation.
- Rest. Rest. Rest. Overtired puppies bite and bite HARD. This might mean enforcing rest periods, especially if you can see your puppy getting 'silly'.
- Look after yourself as well, with rest and time away from your puppy too! Keep any cuts and scratches clean and remember that the 'puppy blues' are a real thing – chat to friends about how you feel, especially if you are tired and frustrated.
- Do remember that your puppy is a baby in an alien world with different language and expectations – they are trying their best and we can help them learn about what is and what is not acceptable.
- Wear clothing without grabbable or tug-able belts, sleeves, legs, hems and so on.
- Have handy items/toys that are allowable for your puppy to grab and tug on – offer these to your puppy when they grab something they should not have, including you or your clothes.
- Know that puppy biting does stop with maturity – in my experience it almost vanishes overnight.

Often working spaniels find themselves looking for a new home because of retirement, an injury or because they have not met the required grade for competition. These dogs often have exceptional basic training and relish the opportunity to become family members, sometimes with the benefits that do not always come with being a working spaniel.

The downside to rehoming an older dog is that you might not know everything about their background and history, including health. If you have small children, make sure that their initial interactions with an older spaniel are carefully managed and supervised initially, especially if the dog is not familiar with children. This also applies to interactions with other animals such as cats, too!

However, I have had the pleasure of working with many rehomed spaniels and have rehomed two myself, who have been loved and fabulous family members. Do not discount an older dog joining you, especially if the prospect of a new puppy fills you with dread.

TOP TIPS FOR CHOOSING YOUR SPANIEL

- Do your research on what spaniel breed or type will be best suited to your lifestyle in terms of size, activity level, grooming needs and personality.
- Speak to others living with spaniels and ask all about their experiences, good and maybe not so good!
- Be prepared to wait for the right spaniel to join you – good breeders often have long waiting lists – do not rush or feel pressured into deciding and if a situation does not feel right, walk away.
- If you are rehoming a spaniel, make sure you know as much about their history as possible and try to maintain as much familiarity and routine as possible – this will help them feel safe, welcomed and to integrate as quickly as possible.
- Start as you mean to go on, whether you have an eight-week-old puppy or an older rehomed spaniel – clarity and consistency of expectations (from all members of your household!) will help your spaniel settle into your routine.

Many working dogs enjoy the benefits of household living, especially in retirement.

Rehoming an older spaniel can bring the joy of a spaniel into your life without the stress of a new puppy.

CHAPTER

SPANIEL CARE AND TRAINING – FROM PUPPY TO SENIOR

Care and training are integral to sharing your life with a spaniel. With good day-to-day care and management, you can help keep your spaniel happy and healthy. Training is critical to hone and harness your spaniel's inbuilt abilities. Training also ensures your spaniel is a canine good citizen and a pleasure to live with, rather than an out-of-control, long-eared, destructive menace.

Care considers nutrition, exercise, housing and healthcare, while training encompasses how, when and what we teach our spaniel in order to ensure a harmonious relationship with clear and respectful expectations and boundaries at home and away.

This chapter covers essential spaniel care and management. Life stages will also be considered, including

Care and management are integral to supporting a good life for your spaniel.

some of the associated changes and challenges, what to expect and how to manage them.

SPANIEL HEALTHCARE

Like all dogs, spaniels have healthcare needs. Spaniels might be considered at slightly higher risk of accidental injuries as a result of their active (and occasionally impulsive) natures, so a comprehensive first aid kit is a good idea, as well as having your vet's contact details (including out of hours) handy at all times for illnesses and injuries. Insurance for veterinary fees can make the difference between being able to have treatment or having to make a difficult decision.

What follows highlights those health concerns of particular relevance to spaniels, including routine and preventative healthcare.

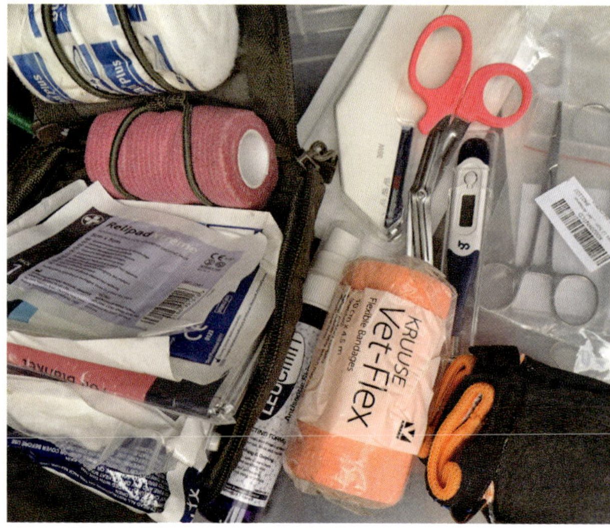

A first aid kit is an essential part of spaniel care.

Ear issues

The pendulous ears of spaniels can mean that ear infections or foreign objects in ears are common. Routine use of ear cleaners is not recommended for otherwise healthy dogs, but do check ears regularly and if they appear dirty (often a thick brown, greasy wax) then a clean and vet check might be in order. Avoid poking anything into the ear canal, especially if you suspect a foreign body, as this can simply push it in further and create other issues. Snoods and hoods can be purchased for your spaniel to wear around their ears if this is a concern and many spaniels accept them quite happily.

If your spaniel starts head shaking and holding their head to one side, this is often a sign that a grass seed or similar has made its way into the ear canal. Avoid 'waiting to see' and seek veterinary assistance, as prompt removal is essential. Ears are really painful if sore. Even the most tolerant spaniel can be upset and redirect aggressively if a sore ear is touched. Lots of head shaking can also run the risk of a haematoma of the ear – a large blood blister – which again can be painful and difficult to heal.

Snoods can be useful to keep your spaniel's ears clean and minimise foreign body entry.

If your spaniel swims lots and loves water, it is possible that they will get water in their ears. In most cases, a good shake removes this excess water, but sometimes it can lead to infections. If your spaniel does get very wet ears and shakes excessively after being in water, gently towel-dry them. You can even cut a section out of a pair of ladies' tights, fold their ears over their head and pull the tights section over like a head band.

Spaniels that swim or are in water regularly can suffer ear problems.

This helps the ear canal to dry out well. This trick was taught to me by an old gundog friend who did this with all his spaniels after swimming. He swore he had never had an ear infection in his team as a result.

Grass seeds

Spring and summer months can be traumatic for spaniel caregivers, trying to avoid the peril that is grass seeds. Many seeds are sharp and barbed, meaning they get caught in hair and can penetrate skin. This can lead to nasty abscesses, often between the toes or in the 'armpit' or groin. If your spaniel presents with sudden lameness, licking or nibbling at a paw excessively, suspect a grass seed. You might be able to gently extract it with tweezers before it causes damage.

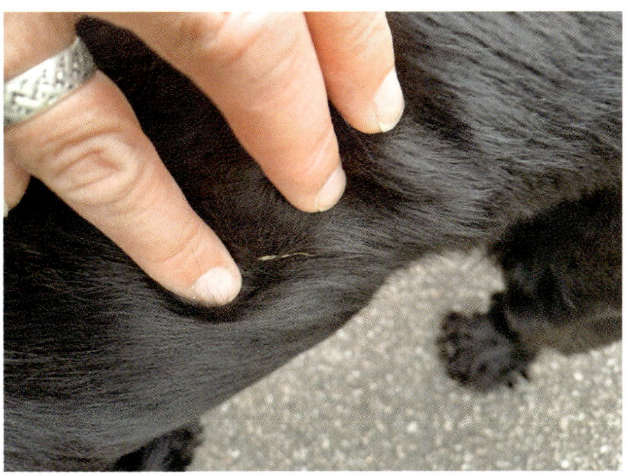

Grass seeds are a particular risk during the summer months.

Alternatively, you might find a lump between their toes where the seed has entered and set up an infection. This will be extremely painful and needs veterinary attention. Grass seeds can also migrate through the body tissues causing significant inflammation, damage and pain.

During the grass seed months, walking in areas with short grass can reduce this risk. It is also good practice to regularly check and groom your spaniel, as this can easily remove seeds that might not otherwise been seen.

Digestive issues

Spaniels tend to be robust and healthy. When fed a good diet that provides the correct amount of energy and nutrients to support their life stage and activity level, then digestive health should be good. Many spaniels are food oriented and not fussy eaters, so present with fewer digestive challenges than other dog breeds.

The digestive system is important for overall health and well-being and contributes to behavioural and emotional health. Supporting a healthy digestive system is important for overall welfare.

Transient digestive illness is not uncommon, especially in dogs that spend a lot of time outdoors and may drink from dirty water sources or consume less than ideal items. Providing that any vomiting, digestive discomfort (often presenting as stretching, 'bowing,' retching, looking at their flank and groaning) and loose stools or diarrhoea is limited (no more than a few hours before resolution) then it is likely that a transient upset has occurred. If signs persist or are accompanied by blood-tinged vomit, diarrhoea, lethargy, dehydration, and your spaniel is unhappy, seek veterinary care. This is especially important for vulnerable young or older spaniels.

Dietary indiscretions and foreign bodies

Many spaniels are very food oriented. If they are not eating food items they have scavenged, they might consume indigestible items – socks are a perennial favourite. Sadly, this can result in emergency surgery for intestinal blockages, so be very aware if you have a spaniel who does this. Watch for the signs of digestive discomfort and seek immediate veterinary support if you know your spaniel has swallowed such an item.

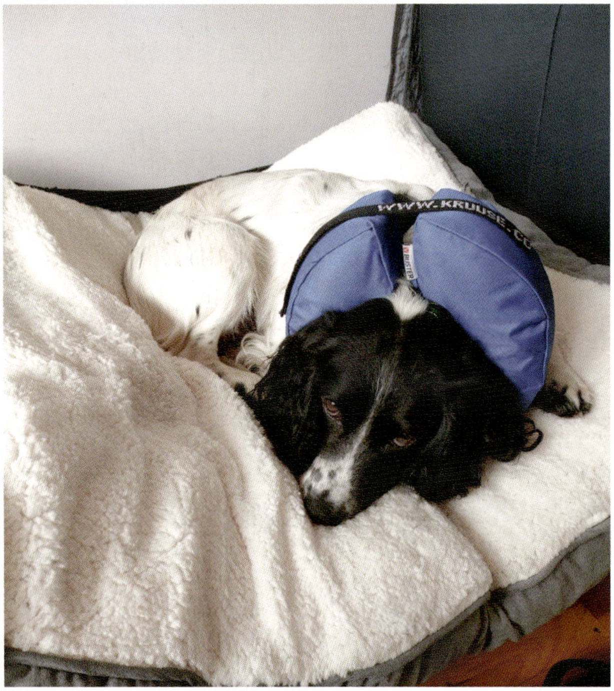

Emergency surgery for intestinal blockages is sadly a common veterinary issue for spaniels and requires extensive, supportive recovery.

With puppies, teach them a simple swap of items is essential to prevent the desire to hoard, hide and often consume prohibited or 'acquired' items. Be very careful with access to items like socks, gloves and underwear that are often prized.

If your spaniel is a scavenger and will eat foodstuff that might make them ill, try some training about self-control around foodstuffs, but also look at muzzle training for confirmed scavengers to keep them safe and well. If your spaniel accidentally eats potentially toxic human foods such as grapes, raisins, chocolate, onions, macadamia nuts and foods containing the artificial sweetener xylitol (including chewing gum and some toothpastes), seek veterinary help immediately, because they can be life-threatening.

Digestive intolerances and allergies

Allergies are rare and tend to be to specific dietary proteins – often animal-derived. Allergies occur when the immune system aberrantly responds to the presence of a specific substance – an allergen – and can be fatal in extreme situations. Beef, dairy and soya are major dietary allergens for our dogs, although it is quite possible for an allergy to develop to any protein.

Intolerances are more common, where the digestive system reacts unfavourably to a food component. Allergies present as serious and almost immediate reactions to the allergen – extreme digestive upset and other signs such as scratching or swelling around the mouth. Intolerances are more subtle, appearing as loose stools, vomiting, general mild discomfort and scratching, often long after the offending item has been eaten.

Working out what your spaniel is either allergic or intolerant to is not easy and available tests are not as robust as thought. A food elimination diet and then a reintroduction of key ingredients is the best way to identify the cause. This takes time and professional input to be done correctly. Alternatively, you might choose to feed a diet described as limited ingredient, anallergenic (free from possible allergenic ingredients or prepared in a way to limit the immune system reacting to them) or hypoallergenic, where the ingredients are less likely to elicit a challenge response.

VACCINATIONS AND PREVENTATIVE HEALTHCARE

Vaccinations against potentially serious diseases are an important part of preventative healthcare. They are generally first given during puppyhood as a series of two vaccinations given two to four weeks apart, the first around eight weeks old. Diseases vaccinated against will differ based on your location and relative risk. In the UK, the core vaccinations are against distemper, parvovirus, infectious hepatitis and leptospirosis.

Optional vaccinations can be given for protection against kennel cough and rabies if your dog is travelling. 'Booster' vaccinations are then given on a routine basis (annually for some diseases and every three years for others) or as needed, based on 'titre tests', which check the levels of antibodies against specific diseases. If the levels of antibodies have dropped, then a 'booster' vaccination is suggested.

There remains ongoing discussion about vaccination and the types of vaccines used. Dogs can have adverse reactions to vaccinations, but this is rare in the context of the numbers of dogs vaccinated. It is sensible to monitor your spaniel carefully after vaccination. If they are under the weather when a vaccination is due, postpone until they are fighting fit again. If you are concerned, your vet is best placed to advise and support you in your choices.

PARASITES AND THEIR CONTROL

Parasites are grouped into those found inside their host (endoparasites) and those found on their host's surface (ectoparasites). Typical endoparasites affecting our dogs are nematodes (roundworms) and cestodes (tapeworms). Many endoparasites are spread by faecal-oral route of transmission. Your spaniel might ingest parasite eggs or larvae from the environment, from contaminated food, or by eating the faeces of other animals.

Others are spread via biting insects or intermediate hosts such as slugs and snails. Some cestodes are spread via fleas. Basically, if you have a tapeworm problem (usually identified by the visible presence of tapeworm segments around the anus – they look like grains of rice) then you probably have a flea problem. If you feed raw meat, advice to minimise parasite spread is to source the meat carefully and freeze it before feeding.

Fleas, ticks, mites and lice

Fleas, ticks, mites and lice can cause intense irritation and can spread other diseases. Ticks can spread Lyme disease. In places with a large sheep or deer population, ticks are common passengers on your spaniel. Always check carefully after walking. Invest in tick remover tools and keep them handy so you can remove any ticks as soon as they are found. Do not be tempted to pull a tick out by hand, smother it with creams or oils, or burn it.

If you remove a tick, pop it in a labelled container, freeze it and monitor the tick bite site carefully. Should a red, inflamed 'bullseye' pattern appear around the bite site, then seek veterinary advice. The retained tick can then be checked for presence of any disease-causing organisms.

Ticks should be removed as quickly as possible using a tick remover tool.

Control of ectoparasites involves environmental management. If you have a flea problem there will also be a population happily living in your home, carpets and car. If you share your home with a cat, be aware that fleas can hop from cat to dog and vice versa, so parasite control is important for both species.

Mites and lice are less of an issue unless your spaniel is regularly exposed to wild animals and their habitats. Harvest mites are a concern during autumn and winter months in specific locations – often woodland. These small, orange-coloured mites might be found on dogs' paws after walking in and, for some dogs, can cause significant illness. If they are a concern in your area, chat to your vet about preventative measures to minimise risk. If you do walk your spaniel in affected areas, groom and examine them for mites afterwards.

Faecal Egg Counts

Many caregivers now collect faecal samples from their dogs and send these samples to specialised laboratories for faecal egg counts (FECs) to check for endoparasites.

Because many anti-parasite treatments can be harmful to the environment, FECs are a sensible way to manage parasite burdens in an informed way and permit treatment based on actual rather than potential need. Parasites and their eggs are very small and cannot be easily seen with the naked eye, so you might not know that your dog has a problem without FECs. Indeed, you will only rarely see parasites in faeces, often only after using an effective de-wormer. Just because you do not see worms, do not assume your dog does not have them.

'Natural' parasite control

Be cautious of apparent 'natural' methods of parasite control that claim to be 'chemical-free'. These methods are not validated for efficacy or safety. Nor are they 'chemical-free' because everything is a chemical. Furry animal-origin chews such as rabbit ears are often (incorrectly) described as 'natural de-wormers' without supporting evidence. If furry animal parts were effective de-wormers, wild carnivores would be free of parasites – this is not the case at all.

Puppy parasite control

Puppies are at enhanced risk because the nematode, *Toxocara canis*, spreads to them via the placenta and maternal milk. Good breeders will ensure bitches are on a suitable parasite control regimen before mating and during pregnancy and lactation. This supports puppy health, but antiparasitic measures are also important for growing puppies from approximately two weeks of age until about a year old. Some dog parasites, including *T. canis*, can be transmitted to humans, by exposure to soil contaminated with infected dog faeces. This can lead to significant health consequences, including eye damage, highlighting the importance of parasite control and management measures. For the control and treatment of any parasite, veterinary guidance is recommended.

Furry chews of animal origin are not effective de-wormers.

SPAY AND NEUTER

Unless you intend to breed your spaniel, you might decide to limit their reproductive capacity through spaying, where all or part of the female reproductive system is surgically removed, or castration, where the male's testicles are surgically removed. There are also options for vasectomies for males, which limits their reproductive ability but retains their testicles, or 'chemical castration' where an implant inhibits normal hormonal function. The implant is a good option if you are considering castration but have concerns about how your dog might be affected. It is reversible and effects wear off after a few months, so is useful for temporary reproductive management, or to assess the impact of castration. It also significantly shrinks your dog's testicles, which can make recovery from castration easier.

Why consider spay/neuter?

For a physically and behaviourally mature dog, spay/neuter should have little impact on them. It is useful if you have a mixed sex household and are concerned about reproductive accidents. You may wish to avoid some of the challenges that come with having an intact dog – regular seasons for bitches can be inconvenient and, long term, there are potential health risks for unspayed bitches who have not had puppies. For our boys, there are health risks, often related to their prostate, as they get older and if they are not neutered.

Equally, many dogs live their entire lives without being spayed or neutered and are perfectly healthy. Some health conditions are also seen at higher frequencies in spayed and neutered dogs. Always seek professional advice for your own dog and situation to decide what is the most suitable option. We have moved away from blanket recommendations to spay and neuter all non-breeding dogs at six months old and now look carefully at their individual physical and behavioural development as to when is most suitable.

Spay/neuter rarely reduces behavioural issues such as straying and aggression. For some dogs, removal of reproductive hormones exacerbates anxiety, so an individual and dog-centred approach is essential.

Post-spay and neuter, your spaniel's daily energy requirements will be reduced. This means that their daily intake of calories needs to be reduced to avoid the risk of them gaining weight. Reduce your dog's food intake by ten per cent after spay/neuter and monitor their bodyweight to make nutritional amends needed to maintain a consistent, healthy body weight.

Another challenge that many spaniel caregivers note after spay/neuter is that their dog's coat changes. The coat often becomes softer and fluffier as a result of hormonal and hair growth changes. Grooming and clipping is sometimes needed to thin the coat and keep your spaniel comfortable (and presentable!).

SPANIEL NUTRITION AND FEEDING

Canine nutrition is integral to canine health and welfare, supporting activity, performance and behaviour. There is a range of food choices for your spaniel, each with pros and cons based on your dog's needs and your own requirements. Nutrition should always be tailored to the individual dog and their caregiver, taking account of human, dog and food factors. These will include availability, need for convenience, budget and feeding preferences as well as your spaniel's activity levels, health and their other individual requirements change.

A balanced diet for your spaniel supplies nutrients in the amounts and forms that meet their requirements. Their diet also needs to be safe, palatable and acceptable to them and you. Canine caregivers have two nutritional options available – to home-prepare your dog's food or the use of a commercially available option, although you can combine the two.

Nutrients and nutrition

Food provides energy for activity and nutrients to support growth, repair and maintenance of the body.

A balanced diet will be safe, palatable and provide everything your spaniel needs to thrive.

Fresh, clean drinking water should always be available.

Nutrients are substances that can be digested and absorbed and are supplied via food ingredients. While there are many different ways to provide nutrition to your spaniel, it is important to remember that no matter what you feed, it is nutrients that our dogs need. The food ingredients we feed supply those nutrients.

Protein, carbohydrates and fat are all sources of dietary energy. Our dog's diet must meet their energy needs first before nutrients can be used for growth or repair. Fat provides more than twice the energy per gram than protein or carbohydrate and the canine metabolism preferentially uses fat as fuel, making it an important nutrient for our highly active spaniels.

Dietary protein supports growth, repair and reproduction by providing a source of amino acids. These are the 'building blocks' of body structures. Protein is supplied by animal- and plant-derived dietary ingredients, but protein from animal sources is usually preferred by our dogs and is of higher 'biological value'. The quality, structure, amino acid composition and digestibility of proteins differ. Egg is an example of a protein with high digestibility, biological value and overall nutrient composition. Conversely, shoe leather or animal skin chews are protein rich, but not very digestible.

Carbohydrates are a diverse range of compounds, from simple sugars such as glucose (which is essential for functioning of the nervous system and is the end point of all digestion) to complex carbohydrates such as fibre, which our dogs have very limited ability to digest. Dogs have sweet taste receptors, so will often select sweet foods such as ripe fruit. Starch carbohydrate found in many grains can be digested by our dogs, providing it has been adequately processed. Fibrous carbohydrates tend to pass through our dogs' digestive system unchanged.

Vitamins and minerals are also found in food, but are needed in very small amounts. They are critical for normal body function and need to be properly balanced in the diet.

Water is critical for normal bodily processes and temperature regulation, so is essential. Fresh, clean drinking water should always be available because a lack of water will cause problems for your spaniel far faster than malnutrition.

How to feed your spaniel

Nutrition is not just about what you feed – how and when is also important. Twice-a-day feeding fits with human lifestyles, but some spaniels prefer single meals and others might need multiple, small meals.

Leave at least an hour between feeding and exercise to avoid digestive upset. The longer you leave between mealtimes and exercise, the better your spaniel will be able to digest their meals, and faecal output will be of better consistency too.

Your spaniel needs to feel safe and secure when eating – avoid the temptation to interfere with them when they are eating, even for training purposes. Some dogs get very worried when eating in the presence of other dogs, people or animals and can become aggressive. Maintain a routine about feeding and keep feeding and meal preparation areas clean. Bowls and utensils should be washed and scrubbed in warm, soapy water regularly, including storage containers.

There are also many alternative ways of delivering food to our spaniels in the form of scatter feeding, food activity toys, puzzle feeders, and slow feeding bowls. These can help prolong feeding times and add environmental enrichment.

What is the best food for my spaniel?

Dogs evolved as scavengers and have been highly successful as a result. The canine digestive system is that of a typical carnivore. There are sharp canine teeth and the 'carnassial apparatus' consisting of overlapping teeth in the upper and lower jaw that act like a pair of shears. Dogs usually prefer to eat animal-derived tissue and have limited ability to fully digest non-processed plant material. Dogs do not chew their food, instead, they gulp and gorge feed – eating a lot quickly and then resting and digesting. Nutritionally, dogs are described as omnivores, or facultative carnivores, meaning that they can exist on a diet of both plant and animal material.

There are a number of diet options available. If your spaniel's diet is providing all the energy and nutrients to support the maintenance of their body, activity and any other physiological demands (pregnancy, lactation, recovery), they are fit, healthy and happy, then your dietary choices are likely to be effective. Work from an evidence base and beware of fads, trends and fashions in feeding to find the right diet for you and your spaniel.

Make sure their diet is well formulated to nutritional guidelines, which ensure that all the energy and other nutrients needed to survive and thrive are provided. If you are unsure on how to make the best nutritional choice for your spaniel, seek suitable professional guidance.

When should I consider dietary changes for my spaniel?

How your spaniel looks, behaves, performs and even what their poo looks like can give you an idea if their diet suits them. They should have a lean body condition, and healthy skin and coat with no excess scratching or unusual hair loss. Faeces should be firm and well-formed. Offensive odours, very soft or very hard faeces might indicate that their diet could be reviewed. Different life stages and health concerns will need nutritional amends with professional support.

Make a habit of regular weighing and body condition scoring to monitor weight. It can be gained and lost surprisingly fast. You should be able to easily feel their ribs without too much pressure and when viewed from the side they will have a clear upwards abdominal tuck. They should also have a clear waist when viewed from above. If you need to apply pressure to feel their ribs, or they lack a waist or abdominal tuck, then dietary amends and lifestyle changes are in order.

EXERCISE FOR YOUR SPANIEL

Spaniels have been selectively bred for generations as working dogs. As a result, exercise and activity is important – spaniels are active dogs who enjoy time outdoors, exploring and undertaking a range of activities.

If the idea of exercising in all weathers, rain or shine does not appeal to you, a spaniel is not a great choice as a canine companion. If you would rather spend your spare time indoors, an alternative breed (or a cat!) might be a better fit. Spaniels thrive on having their brain and body challenged and physical and mental exercise is critical for their well-being, no matter what the season.

How much exercise is ideal?

A common complaint from many novice spaniel caregivers is that they are walking their spaniel for miles each day, and yet, their spaniel is never tired. Exercise creates a canine athlete and the more exercise your spaniel gets, the fitter they become and the more they will need. If exercise and activity needs are not then met, they can become bored and frustrated. This may result in behavioural challenges such as destructive behaviour in the home.

This does not mean that you should not exercise your adult spaniel, or limit what they do. Instead, it is about finding that 'sweet spot' of meeting their physical and behavioural activity needs, within the confines of your own lifestyle. Balancing mental and physical activity is important – many spaniels rest much happier after they have had both mental and physical challenge. Incorporating activity into your dog's daily routine is important for their physical and behavioural health and welfare. It will benefit you, too!

Spaniels enjoy being outdoors and being active.

Spaniels have the ability to be active for several hours each day. They have inbuilt endurance and stamina, as well as the enthusiasm to enjoy movement, running, play, hunting and retrieving. Recognising that you are bringing a dog into your home who will enjoy and thrive off regular outdoor activities is crucial.

How much exercise is needed by the typical spaniel? What should you plan for and what should you expect to incorporate into your daily/weekly routine? Like so many things, the answer is 'it depends' on your individual spaniel, your lifestyle and any ambitions you have to work your spaniel or be involved in specific disciplines.

Puppy exercise

Young, growing puppies need the amount and type of physical activity managed. This protects their growing bodies and their joints especially. Puppies under six months of age grow rapidly and if they are exposed to repetitive impact or activity that pushes them beyond their capabilities, then acute injury is possible.

Long-term harm to their musculoskeletal system is also a risk. Conditions such as osteoarthritis are commonly diagnosed in young dogs, not just older dogs. This might be linked to excessive exercise during sensitive development stages, resulting in growth changes or trauma to their developing body, predisposing them to problems later in life.

Think 'little and often' for your puppy's exercise and maintain this approach until they reach their adult size, while gradually increasing the amount, intensity and frequency of activity. Avoid letting very young puppies run up and down stairs – even doorsteps can be potentially dangerous, meaning you might want to carry your puppy in and out initially. Jumping into and out of vehicles or on/off high surfaces is to be discouraged during growth. Even for adult dogs, evidence

Limit jumping onto objects and in and out of vehicles to protect joint health.

Play with other puppies and suitable adult dogs is a good learning experience.

indicates that repetitive jumping in and out of vehicles can be problematic for joint health.

Allow your puppy free movement and incorporate lots of training, especially in those early weeks when they are reluctant to venture far from you and you can reinforce closeness and recall frequently. Avoid long lead walks on roads and pavements – this is not ideal for developing limbs and joints, nor is it conducive to developing good loose-lead walking.

Free running with other similar-sized and aged puppies and older dogs is beneficial for many young dogs, but be alert to any extreme behaviour, bullying or your puppy becoming uncomfortable. Many adult dogs are not very tolerant of puppies and can be quite mean to them in some cases. Ensure positive and pleasant interactions with other dogs as part of your puppy's ongoing social development. If in doubt, always stop play for everyone's safety and sanity. This also applies to playing with children, where safety for all is paramount.

Beware the weekend warrior spaniel

Spaniels run the risk of becoming 'weekend warriors' – being sedate Monday to Friday and then going marathon running at the weekend. The chances are that they will happily do this, but without regular conditioning and maintenance of fitness, this routine can lead to injury and other health issues.

Try to maintain a regular level of consistent exercise and activity duration and intensity. This can help keep your spaniel fit, active and healthy into their later years.

TRAINING

Part of the care and management of your spaniel is training them. Dog training has moved on significantly from the domineering, punitive and downright harsh methods that were once common. It is now clear that effective dog training results from motivation and reward. Because spaniels can be incredibly sensitive, kind, fair and empathetic training goes a long way to making it pleasurable for dog and handler as well as ensuring effective and functional outcomes.

Training should also be a lifelong habit. Skills and behaviours should be regularly practised and reinforced, especially important ones like recall (*see* Chapter 7). Spaniels thrive on learning new skills and training helps maintain a partnership between you and your spaniel. People often ask when they should start training their spaniel, and sometimes when they can stop. Training can start as soon as your puppy comes home and even our senior spaniels can learn new tricks!

Choosing a trainer or training class

Professional training support and advice is a good idea, even if you are an experienced spaniel person. For socialising a young puppy and exposing them to the wider world, training classes are really beneficial. If you have ambitions to become involved in specific activities (*see* Chapter 9) then specialised classes will ensure you train in line with current regulations and competitive needs.

To choose a trainer or training class, look for suitable experience and qualifications and accreditations from a reputable organisation. Ask about the training methods used and find out about the class structure and expectations. You and your dog must be happy and comfortable in any training situation. If at any time you are uncomfortable, walk away.

Be wary of classes with lots of dogs and if there are 'free play sessions' as integral parts of the class. If there are dogs of different ages and sizes, this can be a recipe for disaster if not carefully managed. Equally, know that while your spaniel might behave like an angel at home, they may regress significantly in the realms of a highly arousing and exciting training class. Good trainers will always work with you and your spaniel to make exercises suitable and achievable without distress. Indeed, training should be motivational and fun for all concerned and a way of developing robust skills for life.

Even senior spaniels can learn new tricks and keep up with training.

CREATING A GOOD LIFE FOR, AND WITH YOUR SPANIEL FROM PUPPY TO SENIOR

While different dog breeds each have typical, average lifespans, most spaniels live for around thirteen years. Some will be visibly 'old' earlier than others, while others are almost 'Peter Pan'-like and barely appear to age. Indeed, one common trait with many spaniels is that they often remain active and alert as they age, if otherwise healthy.

Typical canine life stages include puppy (birth to around twelve months), junior (12–24 months), adult (two to seven years) and senior (seven years plus). These ranges do vary for individual dogs, and I know many seven-year-old spaniels who can hardly be considered as seniors and some puppies who are teenagers at six months. Life stages benefit from specific awareness of health, care, training and management needs.

PUPPYHOOD (FROM BIRTH TO TWELVE MONTHS)

During early puppyhood, your spaniel is like a sponge, constantly learning and soaking up experiences. Sometimes those experiences and learning opportunities are positive and beneficial, sometimes they can result in less-than-desirable behaviours. Your puppy is learning all the time. If you manage their behaviour and experiences during this critical learning period, you can go a long way towards minimising the development of undesirable behaviours.

Ensuring positive interactions with people, other dogs, animals and environmental socialisation is also critical, especially during the first six months. There are also distinct 'fear periods', in which your puppy may lose confidence and can be quite worried about the world. The timing of these can differ on an individual basis, but typically occur around eight to twelve weeks old, and then during adolescence. I find many spaniel puppies have a 'spooky' period around five to six months old, 'spooking' at things they were previously happy with. If you see changes in your puppy's behaviour to situations that previously were not a concern, reassure and support them. We can help puppies to build confidence and resilience for their future lives.

A new puppy and resident older dog make friends.

This is Joey and Molly, two spaniels who used to work together, still active, and happy in their retirement.

Teething

Puppies have sharp teeth and use them. Mouthing can be severe and is especially bad when puppies have not learned bite inhibition from their dam and siblings. Tired and frustrated puppies will mouth excessively

This spaniel puppy has an exciting life ahead of her, so positive early experiences are important.

and when restrained and they feel uncomfortable. Pulling away from a bitey puppy often makes it a game (and can damage your skin/clothing in the process). Remaining calm and gently restraining the puppy from further biting while offering a suitable alternative (soft toy or chew, for example) to bite on is a good start to limit their teeth contact on your skin.

Puppy nutrition and feeding

Spaniels grow quickly and their nutrition needs to support this. They are also highly active, so need energy to fuel that growth and activity. From birth to weaning, puppies are depending on their mother's milk for nourishment and that early nutrition is critical to support ongoing health. At weaning, the transition to solid foods means there is a period of digestive adaption and exploration of new textures and tastes.

The move to a new household can be stressful and disorienting for a young puppy. This combined with exposure to a new environment can result in digestive upset, especially if their diet is changed dramatically. Maintain a similar diet and feeding plan as their breeder, at least for the first week to minimise digestive upset. Any required diet transitions can then be made gradually, over seven to ten days.

Puppies are usually fed multiple meals per day. The meal number and amount fed is reduced as they grow to maintain a healthy, mature bodyweight that becomes consistent into adulthood. There are no hard and fast rules, but I usually recommend feeding the daily amount as four meals per day until four months of age when it drops to three meals. At nine to twelve months old a transition to two meals works well. As always, each dog is an individual and this varies for each situation.

ADOLESCENCE (12–24 MONTHS)

Adolescence is when our spaniels become teenagers – they might become stroppy, hormonal and show regression in behaviours. Training can become

Reassure and support puppies when they are learning about the world.

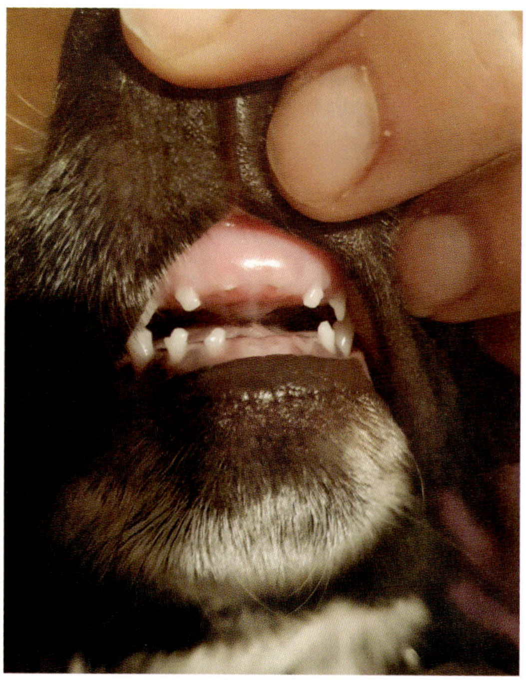

Puppies start losing their teeth at about sixteen weeks old and the front incisors are usually first to go.

From birth to weaning, puppies are dependent upon their mother for milk.

The adolescent spaniel can be a bit of a clown and appear to 'forget' previous training.

trickier and the teenage spaniel 'forgets' how to do certain things. There might also be periods of unusual fearful behaviour. Sometimes puppyhood to adult is smooth and simple, but there are biological changes that we should be aware of during this time.

Most spaniels reach their adult height at around nine months, developing muscle mass and other physical maturity beyond this stage. This means that growth and development still need nutritional support. Intense, high impact activity such as jumping and complex athletic moves should be limited. Usual advice is to wait until dogs are between twelve and eighteen months before looking to undertake serious training for disciplines such as agility or canicross. Indeed, competitively in many disciplines, dogs must be at least eighteen months old to compete.

Spaniel 'puberty'

During adolescence, spaniels become sexually mature. Males will start cocking their leg around six or seven months old. This is also when hormonal surges start, especially testosterone, which can increase male dogs' interest in other dogs, especially females. Your once cute chunky boy suddenly finds the local lampposts and street corners far more interesting than you and they might start posturing with other dogs. This is part of normal development and providing there are managed and positive encounters, most adolescents will develop effective and appropriate social skills.

Females will also have hormonal changes and, based on their overall development, will have their first 'season' anytime from about six months old onwards. It is common for lean, active spaniels to not have their first season until twelve to eighteen months old, in my experience. Hormonal signalling is partly dependent on their body composition and development, especially body fat deposition, but there are also genetic links too. Daughters of bitches who had late first seasons, also tend to have a late first season. The frequency of seasons is individual. Some girls have a season every six months, while others fluctuate. External factors can also affect the hormonal changes in bitches – weight changes, activity, household changes or illness can all delay an expected season.

The first season – what to expect

When a bitch is 'in season' it means she is preparing to be sexually receptive. A season usually lasts for 21 days. The first signs are swelling of the vulva and your bitch will lick and clean herself more. You might have seen her start to increase urination frequency and scent mark too. A bloody discharge on floors and bedding is then seen, but do not rely on this, as some bitches keep themselves scrupulously clean. Put an old light-coloured towel on her bedding to monitor any discharge so that you can accurately time when the season has started (and finished).

During their season, some bitches are withdrawn and lethargic, preferring to do little. Others show absolutely no change at all. Sometimes there is digestive upset, including vomiting and diarrhoea.

When a bitch starts her season, she might be a little more interesting to other dogs, but until around day ten to fourteen after discharge first appeared, she is not receptive to males. Keep her under close control and supervision when in season. Determined bitches will escape and seek a male, but more commonly, determined males will seek out a bitch in season. Unplanned puppies are not a good idea. Her fertile and receptive time is around the middle of her season, and this is when she is most interesting to males. She might even show unusual behaviour at home, mounting and humping bedding, other dogs and even people if given the chance. Once a bitch has finished her season, giving her a bath is helpful to remove any residual odour, before resuming normality.

Adolescent nutrition and feeding

The adolescent spaniel needs nutrition to support growth and activity. Meal number will have decreased and there might be transition to a junior or adult diet with lower energy (fewer kilocalories), lower protein and lower fat content than a puppy diet. Consider transition when bodyweight is stable, and growth is complete.

Keeping a healthy, lean bodyweight during adolescence is beneficial for your spaniel's future health and welfare. When transitioning to an adult diet, do so over at least a week to allow the digestive system and metabolism to adapt.

The mind of an adolescent spaniel

During adolescence, many spaniels regress behaviourally. Recall might become poor and if there has been the opportunity to self-hunt then hunting can become problematic. Revisit and review basic training. Limit your spaniel's freedom, especially if there have been any recall failures or self-hunting episodes.

As with teenage humans, adolescence can be a tricky period when living with a spaniel. With understanding as well as good management and awareness of the environment and internal biological changes, you can survive the adolescent spaniel. Equally, if you feel you need help and advice, seek support – you will not be alone.

ADULTHOOD (FROM 24 MONTHS TO 7 YEARS)

Adulthood is when their personality is largely consistent and constant, they have reached sexual maturity and fundamental life skills and behaviours are robust. If your spaniel is fit and healthy, adulthood should be mostly hassle-free and a time for you to enjoy spending time together. Health concerns at this age should

Adolescence is when you might get an increase in 'challenging' behaviour.

be minimal and preventative healthcare and management, including the maintenance of a lean, healthy bodyweight, will support a healthy ageing process.

Nutrition of the adult spaniel

Once physical maturity is reached, nutrition is needed to support daily activity and body maintenance. Nutritional requirements tend to be moderate, unless they are reproductively active, sporting or working dogs who need energy dense diets and additional dietary protein to support reproduction, muscle development and repair. For most adult spaniels, a suitably formulated diet of moderate energy density and balanced nutrient levels will support health and wellbeing.

SENIOR (SEVEN YEARS PLUS)

Many spaniels remain happy and active with limited signs of ageing until much older than seven. The first signs of ageing are sleeping more (and more deeply), slowing down, stiffness and musculoskeletal issues such as arthritis, and hearing or visual deficits. These are often very subtle, and dogs compensate well. Monitor carefully and seek veterinary support, especially for pain management if needed. Regular health checks and baseline blood tests can detect any early problems so that appropriate management can be put in place.

Toilet habits might fail, and they might need more support to get around. Routine exercise needs to account for changed needs and abilities. Ramps and steps can help get into/out of cars or on/off furniture. Older dogs often feel the cold and the heat more profoundly, so cosy clothing in winter and cooling strategies in summer help.

Adulthood is when our spaniels are both physically and mentally mature.

Canine Cognitive Dysfunction (CCD)

Canine Cognitive Dysfunction (CCD) is the canine version of dementia. It can result in our dogs becoming disoriented, fearful, withdrawn and forgetful. It can be distressing for people and dogs alike. Affected dogs often pace, become noisy (even if they were previously quiet), have altered sleep-wake cycles and get 'stuck' in places such as behind doors or furniture. Aggression and fearful behaviour are sometimes seen, and they often become less tolerant of contact from people or other dogs.

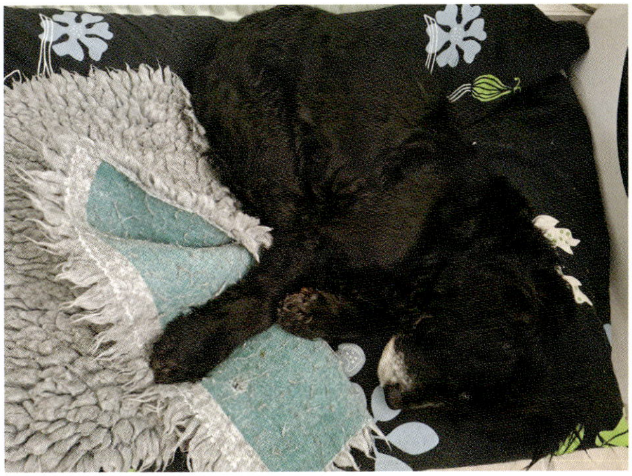

Senior spaniels will often sleep deeply.

Our older spaniels sometimes need a little more care and management to keep them comfortable, including the use of coats and clothing.

A bell on the collar of an older spaniel is a useful safety measure to be able to locate them quickly.

Keeping older dogs on leads or long lines when their sight, hearing or cognitive capacity is failing is essential. It is terrifying how fast they can disappear when out for a walk, because they have become disoriented and panicked. They usually run in the opposite direction to where they came, or where you are – I know, it happened to me and was terrifying, and panic makes them move, fast. A bell on their collar or harness is a good idea so that you know where they are at all times.

Vestibular Syndrome

Vestibular syndrome is a neurological condition similar to a human stroke, where balance is affected, sometimes seriously and causes a range of other effects such as a head tilt, vomiting, inability to stand, disorientation, circling and eye flicking. A vestibular attack often happens overnight or in response to an exciting/stressful situation. Veterinary support is recommended – there are treatments that can support affected dogs, and some signs resolve over time. Sadly, attacks often become more frequent, so careful monitoring is essential as they can be distressing for both dog and caregiver.

Nutrition of the senior spaniel

Older spaniels often benefit from slightly amended nutrition, especially increased levels of antioxidants, and omega-3 fatty acid supplementation to support joint and cognitive health.

Dental health is sometimes poor so offering softer food is a good idea – this might also be more palatable too. This can encourage food intake where cognitive changes might affect normal eating behaviour. Raised bowls are also beneficial if there are joint or mobility issues making lowering their head painful or difficult.

Most spaniels do not need significant dietary changes until health or activity levels alter. Formulated senior diets are lower in protein and fat than standard adult diets and can be useful for weight management. Ageing can mean that digestion is less efficient and increased levels of fat and protein might be needed to counteract the ageing process and ensure adequate dietary energy is supplied.

Sarcopenia is common in older dogs and is where lean muscle mass is lost. Regular exercise and good quality nutrition, especially protein, can help to mitigate this. Similarly, senior dog diets used to have significantly lower levels of protein, as this was thought to reduce the risk of kidney disease. This is now known not to be the case – unless a dog has significant impairment in their kidney function, dietary protein does not need to be restricted.

Euthanasia

Euthanasia is sadly an important part of sharing our lives with animals. It is rare for our spaniels to pass away gently or in their sleep. A difficult decision often has to be made in an emergency or planned situation. It is worth being aware of what to expect.

Euthanasia is a humane way of supporting a 'good death'. Despite the sadness, it is a good way to provide relief and release in the event of severe illness, injury or the consequences of age-related decline.

Making the decision and knowing when the correct time is, is difficult and heartbreaking. Older dogs often have good days and bad days, so planning becomes an emotional rollercoaster. A common refrain is that a week too early for the decision is better than a day too late, although every individual dog-caregiver situation and relationship is unique. You must do what feels right for you and your spaniel.

Euthanasia can be done at your veterinary surgery, or some vets offer an 'at home' service. Your vet will administer medications to sedate and then euthanise your dog via a catheter in their leg. It is calm and peaceful. Your dog will visibly relax, and breathing will deepen and become slower before stopping entirely.

It is your choice if you wish to remain with your spaniel or not. If you feel that your distress will upset them, then perhaps a gentle and quiet goodbye, leaving your spaniel with caring and supportive veterinary staff is a good idea. Being present can help you feel in control and support your spaniel. I have always found it a huge privilege being able to support my animals during these moments, however upset I am.

TOP TIPS FOR SPANIEL CARE AND TRAINING

- Spaniels do have some common health concerns, especially ears, but with care and management, serious issues can be minimised.
- Preventative healthcare and building a good relationship with a trusted vet are a good foundation for your spaniel's health from puppy to senior.
- Nutrition and exercise are essential aspects of any spaniel's life – make sure you meet their specific needs.
- Awareness of life stages and how they affect how your spaniel behaves, what exercise they might need and how their nutritional needs change can help your spaniel live a long, healthy life.
- Puppyhood is a critical developmental period – exercise and nutrition should be carefully managed to support healthy growth.
- The adolescent spaniel can present challenges – be understanding of them and support their journey to adulthood with compassion.
- Senior spaniels will often benefit from lifestyle changes to keep them happy and healthy.
- Training is something that you can do with your spaniel for their entire life – consider it like continuing professional development – even senior dogs can learn new tricks!

CHAPTER 3

UNDERSTANDING YOUR SPANIEL

You might be reading this with a brand new, eight-week-old spaniel puppy staring up at you. You might be venturing into the 'world of spaniel' for the first time with a rehomed older dog. You could be several years into living with spaniels but want to learn more about them and what makes them 'tick'. This book could also be your initial exploration as to whether a spaniel is the right choice of dog for you, your family and your lifestyle.

KNOWING YOUR SPANIEL

It is often said that a puppy is a blank slate, but this is recognised to be overly simplistic. Any puppy is a result of years of genetic selection and inheritance, as well as their early experiences. For specific breeds, this means that there are characteristics that appear with a high degree of regularity and consistency. For spaniels, there are physical and behavioural traits that are constant. Yes, there will be some variation, and this variation is clearly seen across the different spaniel breeds, but there will also be variation within breeds too.

Puppies are not blank slates and instead come with individual characteristics and experiences.

Physically, some spaniels will be larger than others, have longer ears, more coat, longer legs and so on. Behaviourally, some spaniels will be more laid back and relaxed, whereas others are the canine equivalent of a sports car, ready to accelerate over the horizon in a nanosecond. These tend to be seen at opposite ends of the 'spectrum of spaniels', meaning that for the majority of spaniels, there are consistent trait expectations somewhere between the extremes. Awareness of these traits and how they manifest in our spaniels, means we can be responsive to them and manage our spaniels in a positive way. We can also have a good idea of what to expect when we first bring a spaniel into our lives. This helps us understand spaniels and create a mutually beneficial, harmonious partnership.

In this chapter, we will examine how we can best understand our spaniels, so that we can meet their needs and wants. We will then consider how to be the best people we can be for them and how to create the best environment for our spaniels to thrive in.

Meeting our spaniel's needs and wants helps to create a good world for them to live in.

MEETING THE NEEDS OF SPANIELS

When we talk about the needs of any animal, these are fundamental requirements for survival – the need for fresh, clean water; food; health; companionship and reproduction; shelter, effective rest and so on.

These needs are essential for life and the survival of individual animals as well as of a species. Legally, these needs also form the basis of animal care and welfare legislation. The 'Five Domains Model' of animal welfare supersedes the original 'Five Freedoms' and encompasses these needs while also taking account of the emotional and mental state of animals too.

The Five Domains Model of animal welfare recognises that there are four physical or functional domains that contribute to overall welfare status – nutrition, environment, health and behaviour. The fifth domain relates to the mental state of an animal and how they are experiencing the world around them on an emotional level. This fifth domain

Enriching our spaniel's environment helps support health and wellbeing – a paddling pool is a good addition on hot days.

acknowledges the evidence demonstrating the sentience and awareness of non-human species and also recognises the commonality of emotional states such as fear and happiness.

At the most basic level, we must ensure that our spaniels have good nutrition, which includes access to suitable, nutritious food in the correct amounts and fresh, clean drinking water. The environmental domain considers how and where our spaniels live so that exposure to adverse conditions and discomfort is minimised. Health is all about ensuring good health and minimising pain, illness or distress. The behavioural domain is about ensuring appropriate and rewarding behavioural interactions, with other dogs and also with other species (including us) and agency to make individual decisions (where appropriate). The mental domain considers the emotional experiences of an animal (positive and negative) and recognises the importance of positive encounters on the mental and emotional state of an animal. Awareness of these different domains of animal welfare can help us meet the needs of animals in our care.

Physical and functional needs of spaniels

The physical needs of our spaniels relate to their nutrition, environment, health and behaviour. We must ensure that our spaniels benefit from good nutrition, that their daily environment is conducive to their wellbeing and that their health is maintained. We must support appropriate behaviour through exercise, appropriate access and exposure to other dogs, the provision of space and facilities to exhibit 'natural' behaviours and that we allow choice – for example, where to rest.

The environment in which our dogs live is critical to support their overall health and behavioural wellbeing particularly. If their environment is not supportive, enriching, stimulating and nurturing, then it is quite likely that there will be behavioural fall-out in one form or another. Equally, if your spaniel is exhibiting concerning behaviours, in addition to seeking professional support, assess their environment and critically consider if it is conducive to helping your spaniel express functional behaviours.

Emotional needs of spaniels

It is not that long ago in behavioural science that discussion of animal emotions was taboo. We are now more aware of the universality of emotional states in a range of species. Extensive research is adding to our understanding of canine emotions and how they respond to ours. This is important in ensuring we meet their mental and emotional needs as well as physical ones.

From a practical perspective, we must ensure positive emotional experiences for our spaniels and reducing or eliminating negative ones. This might relate to how we train them and how we interact with them when they are distressed or worried. A good example would be if your spaniel is concerned about firework noises. It used to be common training advice to say ignore a dog frightened of firework noises because if you interacted or comforted them, you would make their response worse. This is poor and outdated advice. Because fear is an emotion, it cannot be reinforced in the same way as specific trained behaviours. This means that it is perfectly acceptable, and indeed good for welfare, to comfort a frightened or distressed dog (*see also* Chapter 10). Similarly, a young puppy crying from distress during their first night away from their siblings and mum, in a new, unfamiliar home, deserves comfort and support, rather than being left to 'cry it out'.

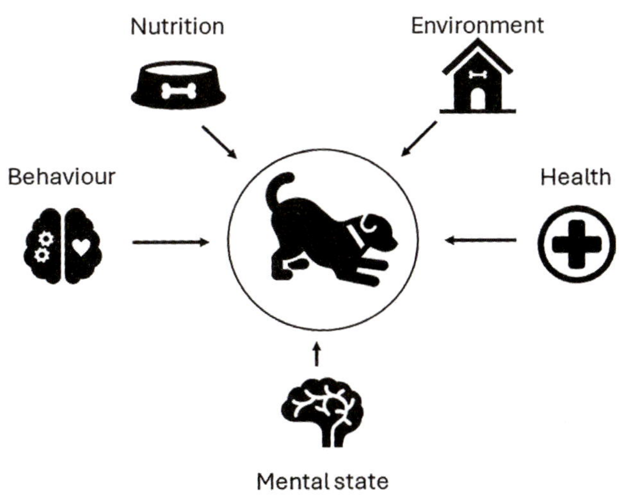

The Five Domains Model of Animal Welfare, adapted for dogs.

Choice and agency are important for our spaniels, including rest places and favourite toys.

An enriching and interesting environment helps support good health and wellbeing, as well as puppy development.

Meeting your spaniel's emotional needs to ensure a positive mental state is also aided by supporting their physical needs of nutrition, housing, exercise, behavioural expression and health. Recognising that many spaniels also tend to be very human oriented (sometimes that interest exceeds their interest in other dogs) is important for ensuring that interactions with people are positive and supportive in all contexts, from training to vet/groomer visits, to everyday interactions with people.

I talk about a 'welfare money box' where you pay into it through positive situations, experiences and encounters. When something unexpected or unavoidable happens such as an unplanned emergency vet visit or a sudden and scary loud noise when out walking, you might make a withdrawal from the welfare money box. If it is full thanks to lots of positive encounters, then a withdrawal should have limited impact and you will be able to address any immediate negative outcomes. If the welfare money box is empty, then this creates a significant emotional challenge for your spaniel and can lead to longer-term concerns that might need more intense training and support. The aim is always to keep the welfare money box as full as possible – this can be achieved by meeting (and exceeding!) the physical, functional and mental needs of our dogs.

Practical ways to meet spaniel needs

Good care and management will go a long way to meet your spaniel's day to day needs. This covers what, when and how you feed, provision of drinking water, appropriate and regular exercise, health care, both preventative and as needed and providing opportunities for your spaniel to express natural behaviours such as sniffing, running, hunting (obviously managed and controlled), retrieving and interacting with other dogs (when appropriate). Training approaches will impact on your spaniel's emotional and mental needs. Using motivational and reward-based training strategies and methods can support a positive emotional state, as well as one conducive to learning – this is good for both canine and human welfare and can accelerate your training aspirations as well as being fun for you both.

Puppies should be comforted and not left in distress, especially in a new home.

The 'welfare money box.' Ideally there are more deposits than withdrawals.

Reward-based training methods help our spaniels learn suitable behaviours even around significant temptations.

Meeting the wants of spaniels

Needs are fundamental for survival and meeting them forms the basis for ensuring good welfare and also promoting a positive relationship between you and your spaniel. It is also important to consider 'wants' too. These are the additional needs of individual dogs based on their individual personalities and the circumstances in which they find themselves, although there are some common themes observed across the spaniel breeds/types.

In talking about 'wants', it is not about giving our spaniels everything they show a desire for. Boundaries and clarity are important and while positive training approaches are recommended, they do not need to be permissive. Indeed, a key life skill is the ability to demonstrate and employ self-control in the face of objects of desire, without frustration. Teaching them that 'good things come to those who wait' is essential. It is also important to teach them that sometimes you cannot always have what you want.

As caregivers, we can recognise individual desires and preferences, permit a level of autonomy (where suitable and appropriate), and incorporate these in our day-to-day life with our spaniels.

What does this then mean for our spaniels and what 'wants' might we need to consider so that we can harness their intrinsic desires in a positive way?

Individual wants

While there are common characteristics observed across many spaniels, it is important to remember that each dog is an individual, with their unique genetic makeup and personality. This can mean that there will be specific, individual preferences and wants.

Dietary wants

Food preferences might relate to what is being offered and when. Some spaniels will want to eat breakfast, while others prefer a single meal or several, but starting later in the day. There will be differences in food type and flavour wants and while I would not support pandering to every whim that our dogs might indicate, an awareness of what is liked and what is not is a good thing. For example, many caregivers get frustrated at their dog's apparent distaste when offered new (and often very expensive) food. Prior experience can impact on our dog's taste and preferred foods. Some dogs will be neophobic (fearful of new things), and this can extend to new foods and tastes. Puppies raised without exposure to different food tastes and textures can also be reluctant to explore new foods. If certain foods have been associated with illness or discomfort, they might be avoided too. Appreciating such individual differences is respectful and compassionate, although, given how food oriented most spaniels are, food refusal is, in my experience, a rare occurrence.

Restful wants

Rest and sleeping are important and indeed essential. I find my own spaniels have specific desires in terms of where they prefer to rest and sleep, the surfaces and bedding they like, and even when they choose to rest. Some are 'morning people' and are up ready to face the world at sunrise, while others are a little reluctant to leave their beds. Dogs are considered crepuscular, meaning they are most active at dawn and dusk, but prior experience, human lifestyle and other factors can impact on how and when our dogs

While there are breed and type similarities, all spaniels are individuals.

rest in reality. They also vary in whether they sleep alone or in the company of others – dogs, humans, or other animals – and this preference can be important to ensure effective and safe rest for all concerned.

Interaction wants

There will also be individual 'wants' in terms of interactions with other dogs and people, including who they actively wish to engage with and who they definitely do not. Dogs are just like us in terms of sociability and not all dogs like all other dogs. Indeed, as dogs mature, their desire to play and interact with lots of other dogs and especially unknown dogs decreases significantly from what would have been observed during puppyhood. The overly sociable dog is actually unusual – they just seem to be everywhere because they get taken everywhere, because they can be taken everywhere!

If your spaniel is super sociable, while it might be their 'want' to interact with every dog they meet, it is highly unlikely to be wanted by other dogs (or people). The overly social spaniel can result in less-than-ideal encounters for everyone. Always make sure that such interactions are mutual and controlled. Indeed, early

What puppies experience during weaning can impact on their attitudes towards different foods as adults.

A puppy crate is a good way of providing a safe rest place for puppies and older dogs.

puppy socialisation is not about interacting with everything and everyone they meet. Instead, it should be about encountering different places and environments and learning to be relaxed whether in the presence of other people or dogs.

'IT'S IN THEIR GENES...'

An important aspect of spaniel 'wants' does relate to what they have been selectively bred for. This means that their genetics do in part drive some instinctual desires, although their environment, training and experience will also have an impact.

Acknowledging the genetic blueprint of a working gundog inside many of our spaniel breeds means we can understand the oft-exhibited 'wants' for hunting, retrieving, being active and having close interactions with their people. Our spaniels have been bred over generations to select these skills and working with them, rather than against them will help you both have a good time. Suppress these 'wants' at your peril!

Spaniels have been bred to be trainable, congenial and biddable – all-important traits for dogs that worked alongside people as working companions. This helps to explain their often-limited appreciation for personal space and their desire to maintain a close contact with their person (except ironically when there is something 'more interesting' at hand!).

Spaniels have also been bred for strong hunting and retrieving skills, which explains their sometimes-overwhelming desire to get their nose near the ground to sniff, and why sometimes those sniffs appear to take over. If you have ever exclaimed that when their nose is working, their ears stop, then there is actually science that confirms this. It appears that the part of the brain responsible for collating scent information is effectively 'switched on' when sniffing, to the detriment of other parts of the brain.

The retrieving desire might manifest itself in carrying items around the house and garden or picking up items when out walking. Occasionally these items are not things we want our spaniels to pick up, so training a robust retrieve-to-hand is essential but also functional – your spaniel happily finding and bringing your shoes can be a fun party trick that feeds into their instinctive behaviours and that they will find deeply rewarding. I even have a litter-picking spaniel who actively seeks out rubbish on one of our regular walks, proudly presenting it to me in return for a tasty treat. That particular path is now largely litter-free as a result of my community minded spaniel.

HOW WE CAN BE THE BEST PEOPLE FOR OUR SPANIELS

The domestic dog is easily one of the most successful species on the planet in terms of distribution, but also in how they interact with us. Domestication and selection for those dogs who were the friendliest, tamest, most biddable, 'pretty' and useful, has given rise to the diversity of dog breeds and types seen. Spaniels are a great example of this intense selection, exhibiting many of those highly desirable characteristics.

One interesting development in canine science has been the increased understanding of dog cognition and learning, as well as a deeper appreciation of the human-dog relationship and the variable nature of it. This has meant that management and training approaches have evolved, particularly with enhanced expectations in how we interact with our dogs and the nature of the relationships we have with them. More so now than ever, we recognise dogs to have rich emotional lives and how this affects how they deal with the world around them, as well as in their interactions with us. While behavioural science is beyond the remit of this book, we should recognise that all behaviours have a function and are linked to the emotional state of an animal. This can help us understand why our spaniels sometimes behave as they do and also aid us in meeting their needs and wants.

Retrieving is an instinctive behaviour for many spaniels.

Canine body language

While our dogs do not speak the same language as we do, they are capable of significant communication. Body language is a major way by which dogs communicate with each other and we can also learn to read and understand what they are telling us via their bodies.

Body language cues are incredibly subtle, but the more you start looking for them, the more you see them. A typical example is when the hackles are raised in response to a threat, actual or perceived. This is when hair along the back, from the shoulders to the haunches lifts, creating a raised line. This is a sign that your spaniel is concerned about a situation but can also signify that a potentially aggressive encounter is about to occur. If an approaching dog has their hackles up, tail and ears held erect and with a stiff gait, then be cautious for the safety of both you and your dog.

Eyes and ears are also useful indicators of how our dogs are feeling. A relaxed spaniel will often have 'soft' eyes and a relaxed muzzle, with their ears hanging loosely. Conversely, a worried spaniel will have a tight muzzle, hard eyes, typically with the white of the eye showing (sometimes called 'whale eye') and ears held tight and erect at the base.

Shaking is also a useful behaviour to watch for, especially when it occurs without your spaniel being wet. You will often see dogs 'shake it off' after an encounter or situation that was arousing – either exciting or scary. It is a good sign that the situation has passed, and your spaniel is able to concentrate again. I imagine it is something like the sudden adrenaline rush and body chill we get after a scare and our body goes temporarily into a reactive mode.

Watching dogs and their interactions with us and each other is a good way of learning about what they can tell us through their body language. Recognising what they are telling us can help us support them and manage their environment in the best way possible to help them feel safe and secure.

A relaxed spaniel with soft eyes and relaxed ears.

TOP TIPS FOR UNDERSTANDING YOUR SPANIEL

- Knowing the origins and original purpose of spaniels can help us understand their needs and wants.
- Animal welfare covers nutrition, environment, health, behaviour and also the mental state of an animal and how they perceive the world around them – we need to consider all of these aspects and how to meet them.
- Sniffing is needed – those spaniel noses were intended to sniff; we might just need to manage when and where 'sniff happens'.
- Born to hunt – spaniels are hunters, so we need to give them constructive and suitable outlets to hunt.
- Spaniels like to retrieve (or most do!) – this means that almost any item is likely to end up being carried by a spaniel. If you are precious about items, then managing your spaniel's access to them might be important.
- Personal space can be invaded by a spaniel at almost any given time – they like to be with you, so privacy is likely to become a rarity.
- Human company is valued, sometimes more so than that of other dogs – be aware and alert to this because separation-related behaviours can be common.
- Spaniels are sensitive souls, often hidden by outward bluster and busyness – handle them with care and compassion.

CHAPTER 4

LIFE SKILLS FOR SPANIELS AND THEIR PEOPLE

Traditional dog training used to focus on exercises that tested obedience. While this undoubtedly gave many dogs and handlers a wonderful foundation, sometimes it lacked relevance to the real world. Everyday life is challenging, whatever species you are. It is important that our dogs are able to cope with the expectations of daily life and that they can behave in a socially appropriate and acceptable way.

WHAT DO WE MEAN BY 'LIFE SKILLS'?

There has been a conceptual shift towards 'life skills' classes for puppies and dogs. These retain essentials of obedience training but with a more applied perspective and include other skills such as being able to be handled for veterinary care or grooming, being able to be calm and more general skills such as confidence and resilience.

In this chapter, we will cover some of the general life skills that will help you and your spaniel build a happy relationship and demonstrate why they are useful in everyday life.

THE IMPORTANCE OF THE CANINE GOOD CITIZEN

Society expects a lot from dogs and their people. Dogs must cope with a range of intense and sometimes scary environments, sounds, smells and sights. The world is a busy place and can be crowded with people and other dogs. Our spaniels need to learn to cope with what the world throws at them and that we are responsible and compassionate caregivers for them.

We must provide everything our dogs need to survive, but we must also provide suitable outlets for their instinctive behaviours, while balancing this with the many restrictions placed upon them too. Some restrictions are legal or civil. Dog control orders limit when

Life skills such as being able to wait at gates are important for your spaniel and you.

and where dogs are allowed. Other restrictions are a consequence of social responsibility – not everyone likes dogs, wants to hear them or encounter their mess.

Life skills are essential foundation skills for our spaniels. Knowing how to train and apply them is essential for us as caregivers. While the requirement for some life skills will differ based on where you and your spaniel live, your lifestyle and even whether your spaniel works or competes in a canine discipline, there are fundamental and basic skills that will underpin their ability to exist in society safely, happily and well. Awareness of these and supporting your spaniel in developing them goes a long way to a happy relationship, minimising potentially stressful or dangerous situations and promoting a harmonious society view of dogs.

What follows is not an exhaustive or prescriptive list, but a compilation of useful foundation skills for you and your spaniel. These form the basis for more functional skills that are considered in subsequent chapters. Application of life skills will depend on your individual situation. Some might be more relevant than others, but all will help your spaniel become a canine good citizen. For each life skill, a short training plan and protocol is presented. You might wish to amend some of these for your own spaniel, situation and circumstances. There might be additional skills developed while working on these, such as confidence, resilience, manners and self-control.

Recall is an essential skill for any dog.

GENERAL TRAINING TIPS

- The training outlines that follow in this and subsequent chapters are reward-based training strategies. These can be quickly and easily embedded into your daily life (several micro training sessions of two to three minutes per day for example) and result in rapidly acquired and consistent behaviours while also building a positive, fun and respectful bond between you both.
- Use rewards that your spaniel values and appreciates. Food rewards are often the easiest to work with, but toys, verbal or physical praise are options too. If food rewards are not your spaniel's 'thing', get creative about how to deliver their reward and the timing of it.
- For food rewards, use something that is visible, reasonably sized and easy to find on the ground.
- Employing a marker word or clicker that your dog is already familiar with will aid the clarity of your training, making it clear to your spaniel when the desired behaviour is achieved – imagine you are taking a photo of your dog doing the desired behaviour; the click is the camera shutter closing.
- For each training session, count out three to five food rewards into your hand – this is a good number of training repetitions to do before a little break and avoids the temptation of keeping going beyond the point of effective learning.
- Keep training sessions short and sweet – even in a training class, do a few repetitions and take a little break. At home, a couple of minutes is perfect, several times a day.
- Start any new skill training in a controlled/low distraction environment and have your spaniel close to you. They can be on or off lead, but only use the lead for management and control (if needed!), not to pull them towards you or into position.
- If you or your spaniel are not 'getting it', stop and revisit later. Frustration and annoyance in either spaniel or person are not conducive to learning!

LIFE SKILL – KNOW YOUR NAME

Your spaniel knowing and being able to respond to their name is a foundation skill. It means that you can start communicating with your spaniel and make it clear that you are directing attention to them – very useful in a multi-dog household. A reflex to name is also a useful 'check' to see if your spaniel is capable of giving you attention and effective interaction, whether you are about to compete, work or go for a relaxing wander where you need to know your spaniel is listening!

This is one of the first things I teach all my puppies – it is a case of 'if you hear this word (your name), please connect with me' and by connect, I expect eye contact. I do not expect a recall and if they are not close to me, I do not expect them to return to me. I just want them to orient towards me and give me some eye contact. I can then follow their name up with a follow-on cue (which might be 'come') or a release cue to allow them to continue whatever they were doing.

For some dogs, eye contact is aversive and not something that they feel comfortable doing. This could be a result of past experiences or simply an individual preference. If this is the case, looking for an alternative form of acknowledgement might be needed.

Response to name by orienting to their handler and giving eye contact is a useful life skill.

LIFE SKILL – BEING SOCIAL

Being social is not about your spaniel meeting and greeting every person or dog they encounter. That is not actually very sociable behaviour – it is not safe either. Lots of dogs are not confident at being approached by an unknown dog and many people also do not want unwarranted attention from dogs. Socialisation for puppies is really environmental socialisation. This means exposing them (carefully!) to a range of different environments, situations and circumstances and helping them learn appropriate behaviours.

However, being social is important. Your spaniel should be able to acknowledge other people, dogs and animals in the environment but have a controlled and mannered response. Running up to people, dogs or other animals either in an excited or worried state is not acceptable and can land you and your spaniel in hot water. You can aim for a neutral response – this is not a suppressed or shut-down reaction to the presence of others, rather it is your spaniel acknowledging them but happy to pass without direct interaction. If you meet someone and stop to chat, your spaniel should remain calm and quiet beside you.

One caveat is that, unfortunately, less-than-pleasant encounters throughout life can create a situation where your spaniel actively dislikes and worries about other dogs or people. This can result from repeated, unwanted interactions or a single event that had a profound impact on your spaniel. In these situations, consider how your spaniel feels, and manage the environment to help them feel safe and secure. If this behaviour escalates, seek professional behavioural help. One of my own spaniels worries deeply about unknown dogs suddenly appearing in her space as a result of an intense encounter with a large dog, so I now manage encounters carefully. Notably, she is completely relaxed in the working and competition environment, probably because she has learned that in that context, the dogs are highly unlikely to pay her any attention at all.

LIFE SKILL – KNOW YOUR NAME

TRAINING TIPS:

- Initially, show your spaniel a treat and hold it up towards your face and say their name. Hopefully, your spaniel gazes up at you and as soon as eye contact is made, mark (verbally or using a clicker) and throw the food reward – I like to throw it behind them, as it breaks the eye contact and forces them to re-engage.
- Once they have found and eaten the thrown treat, have another reward ready and repeat the previous step. Repeat three to five times then have a small 'brain break' with a scatter feed, sniff or wander, then reset. Aim for three sets of three to five repeats in any training session.
- What you should find is that your spaniel will start to offer attention – with lots of repetition, their name will cause them to look at you.
- If your spaniel is not close to you, if you say their name and they turn to look at you, throw the reward to them (ideally behind them to break the eye contact). This can help to avoid their name becoming a recall cue (unless of course you want it to be a recall cue!).
- Repeat and proof this 'reflex to name' behaviour in lots of different places, increasing the distractions and challenges.
- Gradually fade out having to raise your hand to your face so that your spaniel responds to the verbal cue of their name alone.

WHY IT IS USEFUL:

- You can prefix any cue with your spaniel's name to indicate that the cue is for them – it also allows them time to respond and process any cues given.
- Reflex to name can assess if your spaniel is over-aroused and unable to respond to other cues, such as recall. If you say their name and they can give you eye contact, then they are probably able to connect with other cues. If they cannot do this basic skill, then it probably indicates that giving them time off lead or trying to train a more complex behaviour will need to wait a little longer.
- Reflex to name and training it with positive associations is useful because we often inadvertently use our dog's name in a negative way, for example when we are trying to stop them doing something. This exercise can help to rebalance that.
- If you have multiple dogs, reflex to name makes it clear which dog you are asking for a specific behaviour.

A social spaniel is one who can be calm and sensible around other dogs.

LIFE SKILL – BEING SOCIAL

TRAINING TIPS:

- If you have a young puppy, lots of people will want to speak to them and often want their dogs to 'say hello'. While this is lovely, it can create an expectation in your puppy that all people and all dogs are to be interacted with. When your puppy matures, people are less likely to want to interact with them (the cuteness will have faded!) and your puppy will have lost 'puppy privileges' with other dogs. This means, that from day one, limit such interactions, even by saying, 'that's very kind but we are training our puppy to be calm around other people and dogs', reward your puppy for giving you attention and go on your way, or have a little chat without puppy-centred interactions.
- Every time you see a person or other dog, allow your spaniel to look and acknowledge, but then say their name and take a couple of steps backwards to encourage them to move and re-engage with you. Mark and reward them for engaging with the other person or dog, but then disengaging. This can be practised for anything that your spaniel might show a lot of interest in.
- If you find that the presence of people or dogs is getting your spaniel too excited and they are 'going over threshold' to the point where they are barking, yipping, pulling, lunging or standing on their hind legs, create distance from the trigger. Take your spaniel away until they can re-engage with you and calm down.
- Should you end up with a situation where your spaniel is consistently reacting negatively to the presence of other dogs/people/specific triggers, and this is impacting on the wellbeing of you both, seek professional help and advice (*see* Chapter 10).

WHY IT IS USEFUL:

- If your spaniel can be relaxed and able to be in the vicinity of people, dogs and other animals without getting worried or excited, you can be confident going to different places with them, without having to undertake lots of management.
- For spaniels who are going to work or compete, this is essential because they will be around other dogs and people who do not want to interact with them.

LIFE SKILL – HAPPY TO BE HANDLED

Being happy to be handled is a critical skill that means your spaniel can be easily groomed, health checked and lifted or carried when needed. It is easy to assume that all dogs like to be touched, but many are uncomfortable about being touched in certain areas. Paws and ears can be significant challenges for spaniel caregivers, which is less than ideal, given that these are areas that often need careful checking and grooming for grass seeds or burrs.

ESSENTIAL TRAINING KIT AND EQUIPMENT

When teaching and training life skills, you will need some training kit to help you. There is a massive range of everyday management and training equipment available, some very simple and part of the typical canine caregiver's toolbox. Other equipment is much more specialised and often discipline or activity specific.

Our spaniels should be happy to be handled for health checks and grooming – teaching a paw is a good way to make handling paws easier.

LIFE SKILL – HAPPY TO BE HANDLED

TRAINING TIPS:

- Practise handling and touching your spaniel regularly – get puppies used to being handled, held and gently restrained. When you do hold them, reward them well so that they associate it with nice things.
- You should be able to touch and inspect all parts of your spaniel's body, including their teeth and inside their mouth.
- Paws and claws can sometimes be problematic, especially for nail trimming, so start small and gradually build up.
- Use a soft brush all over their body and make it a nice, relaxing thing to do – sitting on the floor with them and a little pot of treats means you can regularly reward them being happy with handling and grooming.
- If you find knots or burrs and cannot easily brush them out without causing discomfort, cut them out for easiness, especially if your spaniel is worried or unsettled.
- At the vets or groomers, do not be afraid to ask to use some nice treats when they are being examined or groomed – professionals are more than happy to help make the process as stress-free and pleasant as possible.
- Allow your spaniel to say 'no thanks' too – if they look concerned or pull away, give them a moment and try again but perhaps more gently or with less intensity.
- Practise collar and harness 'grabs' where you hold the collar (or harness) but as you do so, 'post' treats directly into their mouth – this helps them to learn that restraint is fine.

WHY IT IS USEFUL:

- Handling is an integral part of living with a dog, so making it a stress-free and positive experience helps you and your spaniel.
- If your spaniel is happy with being held by their collar or harness, that is useful if they need to be held by someone else, perhaps for a training exercise or in the event they have got lost and need to be caught and held safely by someone.
- Happy handling means that health checks or dealing with any injuries becomes much easier.

When in a public place, your spaniel should be wearing legally acceptable identification.

Flat collars

A flat collar is a standard piece of equipment worn by many dogs daily. Collars come in a range of materials and sizes as well as styles and decoration. Because your dog should be wearing identification when in a public place (except in very specific situations such as when working) a flat collar is an easy and unobtrusive way for your spaniel to wear their identification via a tag or plate.

Flat collars can be used for lead attachment and walking when your spaniel is comfortable and confident to walk on their collar. They should be fitted well so that the collar cannot get caught on things or be so loose that your spaniel can back out of it. Equally, collars must not be too tight, and this is something to monitor on a young puppy who can grow very quickly. You should be able to fit two fingers between the collar and your spaniel's neck for a comfortable fit.

Collars are not worn by working gundogs for safety reasons in case of getting snagged on something. Similarly, many caregivers will remove their dog's collar when at home for the same reasons – there are many reports of dogs getting collars caught on handles when unattended at home.

The flat collar is a standard piece of canine equipment to which the lead can be directly attached.

For training, flat collars are preferred to using slip-style or half-check collars or equipment such as check chains that can tighten around your spaniel's neck if they pull and cause damage and negative associations.

Leads

Like collars, leads are standard canine equipment, but come in a range of styles, lengths and also materials. For day-to-day use on a trained dog, a lead of about a metre/three feet long that clips onto the collar (or harness) is ideal for walking. It permits some freedom to sniff and move but is short enough for you to control your spaniel and keep them safe next to roads.

A training lead is a useful piece of kit and can be used every day. These are usually double length but have clips on each end so can be used shortened or at full length. The two clips also mean that you can have two points of attachment to your spaniel – for example one clip on their collar or the front ring of their harness, the other clip attached to the back ring of a harness. This can be a great way of supporting your spaniel to learn how to walk with you sensibly and under control but without pulling them around.

Slip leads

Slip leads are commonly used for working gundogs. They are intended to be easy to put on and take off, so are ideal in the working environment. They can also be useful where a dog might be a flight risk. However, for training, especially on a novice dog who has not yet learned the skills of loose lead walking, a slip lead is not recommended. There is the option of using limited slip leads. These function like a standard slip lead, but are limited on how much they tighten, so are good options if you wish to avoid the extreme tightening potential of a standard slip lead or prefer a slip lead for other reasons (limited finger/hand mobility for example).

Long lines and house lines

Long lines and house lines are wonderful training tools that allow your spaniel some freedom, but still ensure that they make great choices and not rehearse unwanted behaviours. Long lines should always be attached to a harness rather than a collar. This is much safer and kinder in case your spaniel runs at speed to the end of the line. A house line is very light and thin and can be attached to your puppy's collar and left dragging around the house so that you can gently manage them if needed. Avoid leaving it trailing outside or when unattended, when it could get snagged and hurt your puppy's delicate neck.

Long lines are fabulous for training recall, retrieve and proximity work. Used well, there should be no constant tension on them, and they should largely be dragging on the ground. Your choice of length and material largely depends on how you are using them. For recall, I prefer an eight- to ten-metre-long line made from lightweight material, which the dog is barely aware is attached unless I need to use it for management purposes.

Many people worry that they will never be able to stop using a long line, but with lots of proofing recall, check-ins and proximity work, you will find that you can gradually dispense with its use.

Extending leads

The use of extending leads typically attracts a lot of discussion with many commentators indicating that they should never be used. In truth, they have some benefits in some situations. Extending leads work on a reel in-and-out mechanism and can be locked by the handler to limit any further movement of the lead section. They are not intended to be used with your dog pulling along at the very end of the lead section but instead offer some freedom and flexibility of movement for dog and handler. They should not be used for walking next to roads or other potentially dangerous situations because they can fail or be pulled out of your hand. Indeed, the plastic handle and housing can be scary for dogs if they end up bouncing along the ground behind them. Should this happen, dogs often run in a fearful state because 'something is chasing them'. The lead part can also cause quite nasty rope burns for dogs or people who get tangled in them, or if you try to grab the line with your hand. For this reason, avoid using extending leads around other dogs or people.

Situations when extending leads are useful include:

- Young puppies in a public place, but you wish to keep them safe and not risk them interacting with other people or dogs.
- Adult dogs in specific places or locations where dogs must be under control or on a lead.
- Older dogs who might be less responsive to recall or may get disoriented and lost, but who still enjoy some freedom and exercise.

Like many aspects of the dog world, not everything is black or white and the use of extending leads falls into this category.

Harnesses

Harnesses have become increasingly popular as everyday pieces of equipment for walking dogs. Originally harnesses were worn by sled dogs and were designed to enhance their ability to pull weight for long periods of time. Similarly, the sport of canicross uses specialised harnesses for dogs when running with their people.

A training or double-ended lead is useful for training, as it has two potential points of attachment.

The limited slip lead is an option where you can get the ease of use of a standard slip lead, but without the risk of it tightening excessively.

Long lines provide a level of freedom for your spaniel while training, but allows you to manage the environment as well.

The use of harnesses for walking dogs evolved out of concern about dogs pulling on the sensitive tissues of their necks when being walked or during loose lead walking training. Sometimes a harness is preferred because of neck injuries or for additional control. For dogs with musculoskeletal issues, a harness can also aid their movement and provide support.

Harnesses alone will not cause your spaniel to pull, but they can make pulling safer for them because the pressure is distributed over the body rather than simply on the neck. Your spaniel still needs to learn to walk nicely whether you use a harness or a collar and avoid harnesses that advertise themselves as 'anti-pull.' These work by tightening around specific, sensitive parts of your spaniel's body or by restricting the normal movement of their limbs, both of which are not conducive to comfort.

Harnesses should be fitted well, and it is worth trying a few different styles of harness to see which best fits your spaniel. Ensure the harness does not extend beyond their last rib into the soft part of their abdomen and that there is no pinching immediately behind their elbow. The style of harness is also an important consideration. They are available in a 'Y' shape, which has a strap that runs between the front legs and a neck portion that lies against the shoulder blades, or a chest strap harness that runs across the front of your dog's chest. The 'Y' shaped harness is often described as preferred and less likely to impact on movement, but current research suggests this is not necessarily so and that choosing and fitting a harness to suit each individual dog, while also recognising the purpose of the harness, is more important.

Head collars

Head collars are sometimes useful for training and management because they offer the handler more control over their dog's head. Head collars work because they tighten around specific areas of the dog's head when pressure is applied. This creates discomfort, which in many cases will stop the dog pulling into the head collar. However, in the same way as pulling into a collar, many excited or aroused dogs will continue to pull, even with discomfort.

A spaniel wearing a 'Y'-shaped harness.

Extending leads can be useful for certain situations but should not be used simply to walk your dog, especially next to roads.

One challenge with headcollar use is that many dogs actively fight the wearing of them, sometimes causing self-damage from their paws and nails. I have also found that head collars do not work very well for spaniels because they can get snarled up in their ears so, generally, I avoid their use, except in certain circumstances.

If you are going to use a head collar, as a management tool for a dog who cannot wear a collar or harness for some reason, or if as a handler you cannot tolerate an extremely strong, pulling spaniel (I have had clients with back injuries for example), take care to condition your spaniel positively to their use and always use a double-ended lead with them – one attachment to the head collar, the other to a collar or harness.

Muzzles

There remains a lot of social stigma about dogs wearing muzzles, which is a real shame because muzzles are a critical piece of equipment that can allow lots of dogs to live a full life while keeping them (and others) safe. For some dogs, it is a legal requirement for them to be muzzled in public places and it is a sign of a responsible caregiver. For other dogs, wearing a muzzle gives their handler peace of mind and confidence. If you travel extensively, some forms of travel stipulate that dogs must be muzzled – this is common for many ferry journeys. Muzzles can also be useful in situations where pain or distress can cause a change in your spaniel's normal behaviour – an injury needing veterinary attention, for example.

Muzzle use is not always to prevent a dog from biting. For dogs who scavenge or pick up items that can cause harm, muzzles are a literal lifesaver. Sometimes dogs with severe digestive issues will wear muzzles when out and about to prevent them accidentally ingesting items that will cause a flare up in their illness.

For all these reasons, training your spaniel to happily accept and wear a muzzle is useful, so that should you need to use one, short or long term, they will be happy. There are different types of muzzle on the market, from tightly fitting, fabric ones that keep the mouth tightly closed, through to wide and spacious basket-type muzzles. If the muzzle is for an emergency, short-term situation, a fabric, close-fitting one is acceptable, but more generally, a muzzle should not restrict the mouth opening and should allow panting – especially if your spaniel is wearing it for long periods or when exercising.

Seek professional advice for the correct fit of a muzzle and spend time getting your spaniel used to initially popping their nose inside the muzzle and holding it there before you put the muzzle on properly. Even then, start small and only for a few seconds initially, before you remove it. Many of the modern, spacious, basket-type muzzles can also have treats popped through the front mesh, making the process and training even easier.

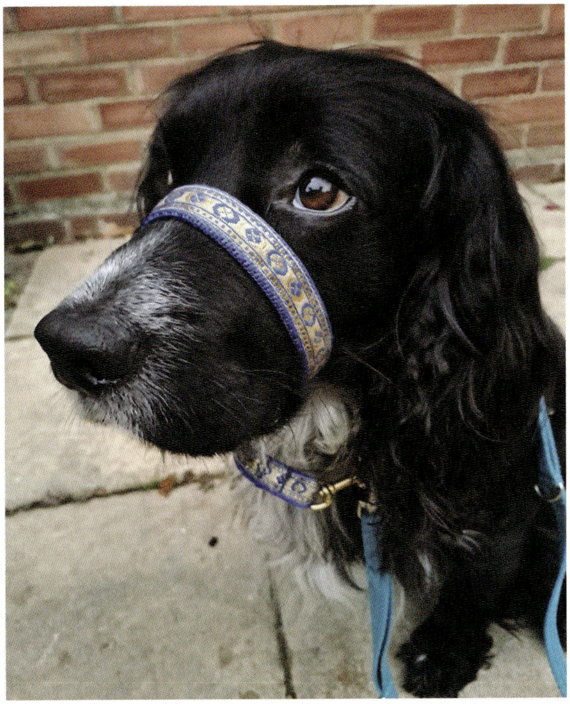

Headcollars are an option for adding control in some circumstances.

TOP TIPS FOR SPANIEL LIFE SKILLS

- Life skills are useful for everyday life as well as building a firm foundation for other behaviours.
- Having effective life skills can make it easier for our spaniels to cope with the challenges of modern life.
- Knowing their name is a critical life skill for all spaniels and should be one of the first things you teach your puppy so that their name is associated with nice things – avoid using their name as a rebuke.
- Being social is nice, but it is sometimes better for our spaniels to be neutral to other dogs and people – this is not being shut down, rather it is being aware of them but having self-control in their presence.
- Teaching our spaniels that being handled, touched and held is OK can help with grooming, health checks and even veterinary visits – cooperative care is where we give our spaniels agency in handling to say 'I'm uncomfortable' but we can help them learn coping skills and behaviours.
- Select training equipment that fits correctly and is safe and comfortable for your spaniel to wear and for you to use.

Muzzles should fit well and provide plenty of space for dogs to pant, especially if they are being worn during exercise.

CHAPTER 5

ESSENTIAL SKILLS FOR THE SPANIEL IN YOUR SITTING ROOM

The majority of modern spaniels will never work as gundogs. While there will be many that utilise their abilities in other working roles, most have long, happy lives as loved companions. These 'sitting room spaniels' might not have expectations of working skills as a field trial spaniel or a gamekeeper's everyday colleague, but they have to meet the needs of their people and the society in which they live – sometimes those needs are extensive with high expectations.

The modern spaniel is more likely to be a companion and family member than a working dog.

THE BALANCING ACT

For any spaniel caregiver, there is a balancing act between meeting the instinctive and genetic needs of our spaniels while ensuring that they are good companions and accepted in the wider world too. Recognising the requirement for this balance can help us develop the essential skills our 'sitting room spaniels' need while also working with, rather than against, their genetic blueprint and natural instincts.

What are essential skills?

One problem is that the essential skills needed for any sitting room spaniel will differ based on their household situation, the environment in which they live and the lifestyle of their caregivers. A family spaniel living in a house with children has different challenges and expectations to meet, when compared to one living with a single person whose entire lifestyle and leisure time is devoted to their dog.

This means that identifying what is important for you will help identify the skills your spaniel needs and can then prioritise their training. For example, you might need to be confident in your spaniel's ability to settle at home quietly while you are involved in online meetings. Your spaniel might need to be comfortable with public transport.

If you live in an urban area, there might be restrictions on off-lead exercise, so your spaniel might need to develop exceptional loose lead walking skills for the comfort of both of you. Other spaniels might need to learn very bespoke skills – I know of one who flies with their person regularly, so training around airports was critical.

Identify the skills your spaniel needs for your life together. Some will be more important than others, and these are the ones to prioritise in terms of training. There are also general skills such as focus, self-control, resisting temptation and frustration tolerance, which are all covered here. This chapter also considers some functional skills that

Self-control is an essential skill all about waiting and waiting well.

The sitting room spaniel often leads a different life to their working cousins.

are essential for the 'sitting room spaniel' and how to develop them. These include loose lead walking, being able to settle and to happily retrieve/release carried items to you.

THE ESSENTIALS

The most basic skills that your spaniel needs are actually general ones.

1. The ability to have and demonstrate self-control/management in the face of exciting or interesting things that might activate their natural and instinctive desires – for example: hunting; chasing birds; carrying items.
2. The ability to focus on a specific task in the face of distractions and exciting things.

It is easy to focus on specific skills like loose lead walking, but forget they are underpinned by more general skills like self-control.

3. The ability to resist temptation, manage frustration and make good choices, even when there are exciting/interesting things that might be preferred.

All of these skills form the basis to developing almost every other skill your spaniel needs, from loose lead walking to recall. The challenge is that sometimes these skills are not the ones we tend to focus on in traditional training, because we want the loose lead walking, we want the recall, we want the steadiness and that is sometimes what we put the training emphasis on.

Working on foundations and incorporating them into everyday life, using them as the basis for every other behaviour, means our spaniels can be active and willing participants in training.

We are training our spaniels to have skills for learning rather than learning skills themselves. Training in this way also means we end up with a spaniel who is more engaged and motivated to be involved with the process, one who will problem-solve and offer additional behaviours and one who is also emotionally stable and resilient to cope with the wider world. If you are in a training class where there is an emphasis on working on focus, self-control and developing the ability to resist temptation as fundamental exercises rather than simply functional skills, then your training foundations will be deep and strong.

Spaniel self-control

For a spaniel, learning that you cannot always get what you want is essential. Self-control is all about waiting; waiting to get what you want and being able to manage yourself while waiting. Lots has been talked about this skill in the education of children and young adults, with studies suggesting that young children who showed self-control when offered a marshmallow had better life outcomes than children who simply ate the marshmallow instantly. Think about your spaniel – are they a 'thinker' who will sit and consider or are they a 'doer' who dives in, headfirst without thinking. The 'thinking' spaniel will naturally have more self-control than the doer, but both will benefit from help in developing their self-control skills.

Self-control skills can be generalised to lots of different places and situations.

An important part of self-control training is making sure our spaniel is in the right headspace or emotional state. If they are excited, barking, whining or lunging, then showing self-control is going to be hard. So, we start simply and ask for micro periods of self-control before rewarding and releasing. This might be asking for a little wait as you pop their food bowl on the floor or asking them to wait as you open a gate or doorway. Start small and with minimal distractions, gradually building up the time that self-control needs to be demonstrated for and in what context – your spaniel should be able to show self-control when still (sitting for example) and also when moving (such as for loose lead walking). Self-control is like a muscle – it starts small and weak but with work and practice, it gets bigger and more effective.

Spaniel focus

Focus is being able to concentrate on a specific task and ignore distractions. The distractions might be noises, people, dogs, wildlife, smells – essentially anything. In training focus, always start in a low distraction environment and reward heavily. This makes it more likely that your spaniel will perform the same behaviour again. You can then gradually increase the distractions in the environment, train in new places and constantly build on your spaniel's ability to focus.

A key focus behaviour to use is the reflex-to-name exercise. Start at home initially – low distraction and low excitement and reward heavily. I then quickly take this skill to new places and practise and proof. Any setbacks in my spaniel's ability to focus on me when asked and we take a step back.

FOCUS IN PRACTICE

I train and compete my spaniels in heelwork to music and canine freestyle. These disciplines involve being on our own in a ring, multiple stewards and helpers moving around outside the ring, judges sitting at the ringside watching us, an audience on one side (which might include other dogs) and music playing. My dogs need to be able to filter everything else out and focus on me and the cues I give. In warming up before entering the ring, I do lots of quick focus tests to check my spaniel is 'with me' – name–eye contact–reward. If at any point I realise that they are not able to connect and focus, I need to do something to help them – there is no point us competing if my dog is thinking of something else! That might be asking for a very easy and self-reinforcing behaviour for them (perhaps throwing a treat) and then seeing if that helps them re-engage. The same principle applies everywhere. If you take your spaniel for a walk to a new location, they exit the car and then cannot even make eye contact with you or respond to their name, their focus is elsewhere, and they will be very unlikely to be able to resist temptation and demonstrate any self-control.

Use it as a test and a way of gauging 'where your spaniel's head is'. If it is clear their 'brain has fallen out', just wait until they are able to refocus. This might be popping them back into the car, moving to a new, lower distraction area or just waiting for them to be able to re-engage with you.

The ability to focus even around distractions is critical for working and competing spaniels.

Learning self-control around food is a useful skill for spaniels and can aid their ability to focus around distractions.

Spaniel frustration tolerance and resisting temptation

Resisting temptation is hard and can lead to intense frustration. Think about the spaniel pulling at the end of the lead, whining and barking at ducks in the local pond – the ducks are the temptation barely being resisted and the pulling, whining and barking are signs of frustration.

We can help our spaniels cope by increasing their tolerance and resilience to situations like this. This is by encouraging them to be motivated to do something else, incompatible with the behaviour that we do not want but one that is more appropriate in the situation.

Offering the opportunity to make a good choice is key here and this is through motivation and reward. For example, 'yes, feel free to look at the ducks on the pond, but then look back at me, get a reward (make sure it's a good one!) and then let's walk away'. You can go back again and repeat until your spaniel is starting to realise that the preferred (and easiest and most rewarding) behaviour is to resist the temptation.

One point of note here (and *see* Chapter 8 also) is that if your spaniel has had the opportunity to not resist temptation, perhaps they have a history of chasing ducks, cats, birds or other wildlife, for example, you will have to do much more work to overcome

Train and practise good behaviour around temptations before undesirable behaviour happens.

Good on-lead skills make walking with your spaniel safer and more enjoyable.

what will have become hugely rewarding for your spaniel. This is where environmental management (leads, long lines, limited exposure, distance) AND training need to be combined.

The more your spaniel practises resisting temptation and frustration tolerance, the better they will become, but it will take time and lots of rehearsing. Early management to prevent occurrences that can become highly intrinsically rewarding is important for our spaniels.

Train and practise the good stuff, long before the bad stuff gets practised.

COOPERATIVE WALKING (NICE/ LOOSE LEAD WALKING)

A dog that consistently pulls on the lead is awful to walk. It destroys any potential pleasure in going for a dog walk if your canine companion views it more as a drag and that you are simply a weight on the end of a rope that needs to be pulled along. Not only is it horrible, but it can cause injury to you and your dog if they are a consistent and powerful puller on the lead. If you have shoulder, back, hip or knee issues, even a small dog pulling on the lead hurts and can destabilise you. Add in slippery surfaces, and it is an accident waiting to happen.

Pulling on the lead is also not great for our dogs. When wearing a collar, there is significant pressure exerted around the sensitive, soft tissues of the neck. There are important anatomical structures that can be damaged from pulling, including the thyroid gland, the trachea, oesophagus and the blood vessels to and from their brain. Training methods that rely on exerting extreme pressure on the sensitive neck of our dogs through the use of tools or specific techniques should be avoided for this reason.

Walking nicely on a lead also means that your spaniel is more 'with you' – aware of you and your movement. Similarly, a dog who is walking far ahead of you is at risk of coming across something before you do – turning a corner into the face of another dog or person, finding some discarded food/litter, or another potential hazard. For all these reasons, having good lead skills is important.

Why do so many spaniels pull on lead?

Pulling on lead is a common complaint from spaniel caregivers. At its most basic, pulling on lead is a result of our spaniels not learning the alternative of loose lead walking and not practising it enough for it to become a habit, as well as their ability to have focus, self-control and frustration tolerance. Spaniels are also optimistic and hugely interested in the external environment. They are also easily distracted. This can mean that they become 'kite like' on a lead,

Using a lead indicates responsible management and care.

rushing from sniff to sniff and desperately seeking their next bit of excitement. This behaviour can become self-reinforcing.

The act of walking at the same speed as we do is also difficult for our dogs too – this needs practice and training, as well as helping our spaniels manage their own body movement to match ours.

There is also the possibility that lead-walking has become unpleasant for our spaniels through the use of aversive or uncomfortable training techniques or equipment. Ironically, pulling can be a sign of our dogs trying to 'fight' that discomfort and get away from it.

Finally, there is also the oppositional reflex effect. Imagine someone trying to push you over. Your instinct is to stand firm and lean back into them. This can also happen to our spaniels when they pull on lead – it becomes self-fulfilling because of this reflex, and we are sometimes part of this process too – the pulling spaniel means we pull too.

Let's talk about leads

While discussing loose lead walking, a reminder about the importance of leads is useful. There is an interesting trend for people to walk their dogs without leads in many contexts. These dogs are rarely under full control. Leads are like seatbelts in cars – there for management and when they might be needed. Yes, they can break, you can drop them, they can be accidentally pulled out of your hand, but the presence of a lead gives you an additional safety net for your dog.

The use of leads is also a good way of showing others (dogs and people) that your dog is under control. Farmers politely request that people use leads around livestock and still some dog walkers think it does not apply to them. I know many people who are wary of off-lead dogs because of prior experiences – this applies to runners, cyclists, horse riders and even other dog walkers. Many dogs have learned as a result of repeated negative encounters with the local 'it's ok, he's a friendly dog' that all off lead (and sometimes on lead) dogs are a potential threat. It is good practice to respect others around you and use a lead, especially when you see an unknown dog, a dog who is clearly showing some distress, or a handler who is trying to manage a situation. For drivers, they can see that you have a connection with your dog and indeed, there are potential legal ramifications of your dog being beside the public highway off lead. It just is not worth the risk to them or other road users.

Being able to walk your dog off-lead might give you a sense of achievement, but it is a skill best kept for situations and places where it is appropriate. Using a lead should not be viewed as a failure in your dog training. Instead, it is a sign of being a responsible, and socially aware, canine caregiver.

The 'lead chill'

The 'lead chill' is an exercise to help your spaniel learn that the appearance of the lead does not necessarily mean something good (or even bad, such as the cessation of the walk) is about to happen. Simply clip the lead onto your spaniel's collar or harness and let them drag it around (never leave them unattended). Practise clipping the lead on and off, as well – too many dogs feel the lead being unclipped and take it as the signal for FREEDOM! You can also sometimes pick up and carry the lead around without going for a walk. This is useful, as often we inadvertently get our dogs excited before they have even left the house. Asking them then to be calm on lead and walk sensibly is pretty tough.

Loose lead walking

Loose lead walking (or even off lead, controlled walking) should be regularly trained and reinforced. One difficulty is that our lives often mean sometimes we need to exercise our dogs without the pressure of training – this is a reality of living with a sitting room spaniel – sometimes you are fighting the clock to get to work on time!

Try not to end up completely confusing your dog or being inconsistent (which destroys learning and partnership). Use something different for 'walks' and a specific lead and collar for training, especially in the early days. A harness and lead are good for what I call 'relaxed walks' – those with no training pressure or the walks that are functional, when you just need to get them out, exercised and toileted. Should your dog pull, then the harness means that damage is limited. I then use a flat collar and lead for 'training' sessions. Over time, the expectation of loose lead walking becomes more robust.

With successive spaniels, loose lead walking is an essential skill I actively work more on now with puppies than I ever have. My spaniels have never been terrible on lead, but they could have been better. I always found training loose lead work really boring, but after a knee injury, the importance of a dog not pulling on lead was crystal clear. If I could suggest one skill to spend time on that will enhance your daily lives, this would be it.

Using a harness and double-ended lead is useful in early lead-walking training.

Training loose-lead walking

Start loose lead training in a quiet, distraction-free environment, off lead. Encourage your spaniel to your side and reward them for being there – do not be in any rush to move. Even drop treats behind you to encourage your spaniel for staying within that zone, rather than moving in front of you (which would be pulling). The aim is to get your dog wanting to be at your side (with their shoulder level with your knee) and to maintain that position. You can do this on both your left and right side. Traditional heelwork is always done on the left but do train on both sides – it is handy for your dog to happily walk on either side, and it is good for their overall movement and physique.

Avoid saying 'heel' to your spaniel before you have the behaviour proofed – our dogs do not come ready programmed to know what 'heel' means. Only when you have some consistent and steady movement beside you should you start introducing specific cues. There is a school of thought that loose lead walking should just become a habit and not necessarily a behaviour on cue. I like this approach, especially as I also expect my spaniels to do competitive-style heelwork, which is not ideal for a walk around the block, and I need a specific cue for that type of close behaviour.

When you are training loose lead walking, make sure that your spaniel is still getting the opportunity to have suitable outlets for exercise – playing, safe free running, retrieving and so on. This will support the skills needed to walk with you nicely and under control, on or off lead.

Start your lead training early, as even young puppies will want to pull to exciting smells.

COOPERATIVE WALKING – AN EXAMPLE TRAINING PROTOCOL

Often the best way to train cooperative walking is off lead so that you are not juggling the lead and your spaniel and treats and maybe even a clicker! Micro training sessions of one to two minutes are often best – they avoid boredom or overdoing it, especially for puppies.

1. Have some yummy treats in your hand closest to your spaniel and stand upright or sit or kneel if they are small and you are at home. Lure your dog to a position at your side with a treat right at their nose and drop a treat on the floor just beside you or a little behind you. Repeat without saying anything (except your verbal reward marker if desired) until your dog is moving to your side of their own accord. This builds a reward zone of being at your side or just behind you rather than pulling out in front of you.
2. Now repeat while adding in your cue – I use 'heel' for my left-hand side and 'side' for my right for close heelwork, but you can use anything you want. Initially you will say the cue as you drop the treat, but try to progress using the cue only to see if your dog moves to your desired position before rewarding. If not, take a step back and repeat and proof step 1.
3. Once they are happy holding a position at your side, take a step or two forward. I like to use a cue such as 'let's go!' so my dog knows what we are doing. If your dog maintains position, drop a treat just behind your knee position again and repeat multiple times! If they bound forward, lure them back to where you want them and reward. Some dogs get confused with the forward movement, so you can also mix it up by moving forward and backwards.
4. Repeat this exercise in lots of different places – boring and exciting. Once it is consistent, start taking more and more steps forward before rewarding. Always be ready to take a step backwards in the training if they start to pull.

REAL LEAD WALKING

One challenge many new puppy people have is the intense desire to GET OUT FOR A WALK! While going for walks is a truly wonderful part of sharing your life with a dog, they can inadvertently produce a pulling puppy. Very quickly, your puppy learns that you tend to go in straight lines to places and that (unfortunately) pulling often gets them there faster. You might have a circular route that becomes a standard walk. As a result, we accidentally reward pulling on the lead or rushing off ahead.

Instead, find a large open space without tracks, paths or anything that means we might be tempted to follow a defined route. Wander, change direction, change your speed, zig zag, do whatever you can to make walking with you more interesting and exciting for your puppy (or older spaniel) than simply walking in a straight line.

There is also an important point here about developing another key cooperative walking skill for our spaniels – their walking speed. Easily one of the most forgotten aspects of loose lead walking is that the normal walking speed of a spaniel is much faster than ours. Part of the training thus needs to consider helping our spaniels to learn to move more slowly and in line with our speed. This takes time and needs physical changes in your spaniel to be able to do this easily.

You can also do exercises and training such as getting your spaniel to step back onto a low platform, to enhance your spaniel's hind limb awareness. This can also help loose lead walking because most dogs are front-wheel drive, carrying more of their bodyweight (approximately 60 per cent) over their front legs. Their hind legs tend to just follow along. If we help our spaniels become more aware of their back legs and what they are doing, we can help them learn to manage their speed and movement to match our own.

BEING CALM AND SETTLED

The ability to relax, be calm and settle in a range of environments is an important skill for all dogs. For

Mix up periods of lead walking with play, free running and retrieving to avoid your spaniel becoming bored.

BEING CALM AND SETTLED – TRAINING TIPS

- You will need a mat/towel or other target – a coaster can be an easily portable target for this skill when you have it solid and consistent.
- Start in a controlled/low distraction environment and have your spaniel close to you. If you can work your spaniel on a very loose, trailing lead, or free, initial training will be easier.
- Pop your floor target onto the floor and let your spaniel see it. In early training, a mat that your spaniel's entire body fits on is easier to make it clear to them what the expectation is – that is, all four feet and your body needs to be settled on this mat, then you will get the reward.
- Drop a treat onto the mat and let your spaniel go and eat it. At this stage, do not worry if they do not get all four feet on the mat. The first step is to make the mat the place that the reward comes from – effectively a good place to be and to eventually stay.
- If your spaniel comes off the mat, repeat the previous step and keep repeating until they choose to stay on the mat, in expectation of the reward.
- When your spaniel realises that the mat is a good place to be and chooses to stay there, mark and reward but this time throw the treat to the side or behind them. This forces your spaniel to move off the mat to get the reward. If they have realised that the mat is the source of the reward, they will come back to the mat and, at that point, mark, reward and repeat.
- Once your spaniel is choosing to go to the mat themselves, you can start adding a cue word such as 'mat' or 'place'.
- With repetition and practice, you can move the mat target around and place it in different locations – you will need to proof the behaviour in different places, but it should start to become a general response to the presence of the mat.
- You can then start to increase the criteria and increase the duration of the behaviour before the reward is given. For example, once they are on the mat, ask for a down, silently count to three, mark, reward and release. Repeat and proof.
- Use food toys to help encourage your spaniel to relax and settle in one place too.

Food enrichment toys can be used to help teach your spaniel to be calm.

Learning to settle is a skill to teach all spaniels.

spaniels this is an essential skill, especially if they are going to be working gundogs or otherwise be exposed to situations where they need to be able to be still and quiet. This could include visits to your local coffee shop, but the ability to relax at home is important too. Calm and settled behaviour means that your spaniel remains relaxed in a range of situations and places, so you do not need to keep managing them. A calm spaniel does not expend extra energy getting excited or agitated in distracting or exciting situations.

Settling can be a difficult skill to learn. The outgoing, optimistic spaniel has to work very hard to be able to choose to remain still and relaxed, observing what is going on around them but not responding until it is appropriate for them to do so. However, it is possible to train and support your spaniel to be calm and settled and it aids the development of self-control and frustration tolerance too.

BRING IT BACK!

A common question asked by many novice spaniel caregivers is how to stop their spaniel helping themselves to shoes, socks, towels, children's toys, tissues or any item they can physically pick up and carry in their mouth. Sometimes this applies to toys in playing or even when you are training a functional retrieve for a working gundog or for other specific disciplines. In competitive or working situations, spaniels are expected to demonstrate a 'clean' retrieve direct to their handler's hand without deviation, mouthing, chewing or reluctance to give the item up.

Most spaniels have an inbuilt retrieve drive and enjoy carrying items. Sometimes they will also carry items when excited or worried, so it can also be a sign of arousal. However, it can become frustrating and even annoying for new caregivers who might be unused to this behaviour.

'How do I stop my spaniel stealing things?'

Stealing is a human construct, and spaniels do not 'steal' for any malicious or spiteful reason. They simply acquire items and then might not immediately return them to us. It is very easy for us to label that as 'stealing', but be assured, it is not stealing in the way we might think.

In its most benign form, this can simply be a funny thing your spaniel does, and, in many cases, they will pick up, carry, and often bring you the item happily. When they do this, it is critical that you reward WELL and give them great feedback that they made a BRILLIANT choice in bringing you the item. This is something to practise with puppies from Day One and build the habit of returning to you and giving you whatever they have. It can also be critical in the event that your spaniel picks up something potentially dangerous or precious. Teaching your spaniel self-control around items and to be happy to give them up when requested is an essential life skill. You can practise encouraging your spaniel to leave items, walk past them and even recall past them with suitable rewards. This is helpful in functional situations where you might only want your spaniel to pick up and retrieve specific items, while ignoring others.

BRING IT BACK – TRAINING TIPS

- Train in a restricted area where your spaniel cannot run off, hide or otherwise get the item away from you. Corridors or hallways are a good, distraction-free place to start.
- Lightly restrain your spaniel – I like to sit on the floor with them at my side and my arm hooked round their front.
- Throw out an item in front of you. If you have a slightly reluctant retriever, allow them to immediately go for it. If your spaniel is rather more enthusiastic, wait until they show momentary self-control and then release them to fetch it.
- When they return, resist the temptation to immediately grab the item in their mouth. Instead, encourage them to come close and fuss them – rub their body, scratch their chest, rub under their chin, while also encouraging them to 'hold' the item in their mouth.
- Take a light hold of the item – using a toy that protrudes from their mouth is much easier to do this with rather than a tennis ball and ask them to 'give' or 'drop' ('dead' is often the gundog cue for this behaviour) and be ready to give the item straight back to them or throw it again as a reward for giving it up.
- With puppies, encourage them to bring you things and swap them for something else – this could be another identical item or something else they enjoy.
- Train being able to give up items on cue using two identical items that your spaniel likes. Have one in each hand – one is moving and encouraging for your spaniel to hold/retrieve, the other is immobile. Throw the 'live' toy and when they bring it back, lightly take it and throw the other one. This toy-swap game is a great way of helping your spaniel to learn to give up items happily.
- Be cautious of using food in training a retrieve, especially if you aim to work or compete your spaniel, as it can lead to them spitting the retrieve item out in anticipation of the food reward!

Train using retrieve items that you can gently get a hold of when in your spaniel's mouth – gundog training dummies are ideal for this.

Work with your spaniel's retrieve instinct rather than against it.

The ability to be still, calm and settled in a range of environments is a useful skill for spaniels.

Resource guarding

Sometimes the behaviour of acquiring items and carrying them or even 'hiding' them can escalate and become problematic. If your spaniel has a history of items being snatched from them or forcibly removed, then they can start to become possessive over them. Often referred to as 'resource guarding', this is a concern for many spaniel caregivers. In extreme situations, spaniels will hoard items and resist, sometimes aggressively, any attempts to recover the item(s). Sadly, many spaniels who find themselves in rescue are labelled as 'resource guarders' – the resources can be anything from litter to toys, to food bowls, and even people.

The unfortunate thing is that we often grab items from our spaniels, especially when they are young, because we worry that they might hurt themselves or damage the item. It takes an impressive level of calm and patience to obtain less-than-ideal items from a spaniel's mouth with aplomb, but it can stand you in good stead and go a long way to embedding confidence in your spaniel to bring you items happily. Naturally, spaniels should be 'soft-mouthed', meaning they are gentle with items – an important skill for gundogs who must not damage game. Careful recovery of items from your spaniel will help to retain this soft-mouthed characteristic.

What follows is less of a formal retrieve training protocol and more functional training tips to support your spaniel in being able to happily give up items. If you are looking for more formal retrieve training and troubleshooting, seek professional training advice.

How to get an item back from your spaniel, nicely and calmly

Sometimes, your spaniel gets something you really do not want them to have. This can induce panic if it is something precious or dangerous. Firstly, keep calm and ask them gently to bring it to you. If they do, again resist the desire to grab the item from them. Instead, lightly fuss them, telling them how good they are but without a focus on the item in their mouth. Clip a lead on at this point if you are close so that you can limit them moving again or hiding. If you have a toy or other item you know they will swap it for, offer that – even consider throwing it for them, as sometimes they will drop an item and go for the thrown item instead.

Alternatively, offer food – from hand or start scattering it on the floor, even over them so they realise that yummies are 'falling from the sky'. Many foodie spaniels will respond with an immediate drop. When they do, pop your foot over the item or stand on it rather than using your hand. This is for your safety as well as limiting the opportunity for your spaniel to grab at the item again. Sometimes, you just need to sit and wait, ready with a great reward for when they give it up; if this happens with an especially desirable item, make a mental note that its accessibility needs to be seriously limited.

Work with your spaniel's retrieving

Retrieving and carrying items is an inherent skill for many spaniels, so we can do so many things to encourage and work with those basic skills and desires and channel them in a positive way. This will make living with your spaniel so much easier and fun. Consider capturing those skills around the house so that instead of 'stealing' socks, they can load and empty the washing machine. If you lose your keys, ask them to find them – training this initially with a suitable keyring that will make scenting and retrieving easier. My own spaniels are charged with finding and bringing me my shoes before we leave the house. They just have not quite learned how to match pairs yet.

Focus is an essential skill for spaniels, and eye contact with their handler – regardless of weather or situation – is important.

TOP TIPS FOR ESSENTIAL SKILLS FOR THE SPANIEL IN YOUR SITTING ROOM

- If your spaniel cannot focus on you and what you are asking them to do, then other skills become much more difficult – work on focus as an essential skill.
- Self-control can be practised in lots of ways – around food, doorways, in and out of the car and so on – this is a key skill that forms the basis of other behaviours such as lead walking and being able to settle.
- Resisting temptations is hard, but we can help our spaniels develop and improve their ability to do so – this also supports the development of resilience, which is critical for everyday life.
- Loose lead, cooperative walking makes life nicer and easier for both you and your spaniel, but it needs work and repetition of the behaviour – make sure that more time is spent walking nicely on a loose lead than pulling.
- Train loose lead walking from the moment your puppy comes home, both on and off lead.
- Being calm and settled in a range of environments is critical for all spaniels; this is a behaviour that can be trained and proofed like any other.
- Carrying items is instinctive for our spaniels – channel it well to maximise a good retrieving pattern and to minimise issues with them becoming possessive over items.

Holding items is instinctive for many spaniels. This puppy is learning to hold and also give up an item using a paint roller, which is a useful training object under supervision.

CHAPTER 6

WHISTLE WHILE YOU WORK

Whistles are often considered to be the mainstay of gundog handlers and shepherds but are increasingly used by dog handlers across disciplines. Even if your spaniel is destined to be an active family companion, a whistle could be a hugely valuable part of your canine kit. If gundog work and training is going to be part of your adventures with your spaniel, then a whistle is an essential addition.

WHY A WHISTLE?

Why might you consider adding a whistle to your training toolbox and day-to-day walking kit? You might already have pockets full of food rewards, poo bags and toys – do you really need something else to remember?

ESSENTIAL EQUIPMENT

A whistle might become an essential part of your spaniel life. Mine are part of my day-to-day clothing and there are days that the whistle goes round my neck first thing in the morning and is not removed until I am settled for the evening. I have turned up to important meetings and lectures wearing mine, they are such a staple part of my daily attire.

A whistle is an essential part of gundog attire.

It could be that you aspire and aim to work your spaniel as a gundog, in which case, whistle use is desirable and preferable to shouting. Game birds are sensitive to noise and even whispered voices can move birds out of areas they are expected to be found in. If you fancy taking part in gundog scurries, working tests or even field trials, using a whistle is expected – indeed, excess use of the voice (and also of the whistle) is penalised in competitive tests and trials.

Whistles are consistent

You might also want to use a whistle for consistency if your spaniel is walked or handled by friends or other family members. Sometimes, introducing a whistle cue for an 'emergency' recall can be useful, and is only used in occasional, extreme situations. A whistle can also be useful if you ever lose your voice and calling your dog or issuing verbal cues is not possible.

Handlers sometimes explore whistle training as an alternative option when it is realised that their existing verbal cues have stopped working for their dog and they want a 'clean slate' to start from. As our spaniels become more mature, sometimes their hearing begins to fail, and they can become less responsive to some sounds and tones. Sometimes, handlers have found that their spaniels can still hear and respond to certain whistle pitches, meaning that communication between dog and handler can be maintained. This might mean that safe off-lead freedom for our older spaniels can be maintained a little longer.

Whistles represent a way to communicate cues clearly and cleanly without some of the inconsistences and challenges of using our voice. Unlike our voice, the whistle rarely betrays our emotional state, which can be useful in situations where our dogs might not respond favourably if they detect we are frustrated, angry or upset via our voice.

Whistle sounds travel

The noise of whistles tends to travel much further than our voice and is less impacted by weather and terrain. This is one of the reasons that shepherds and gundog handlers use them so much – handling dogs over long distances, sometimes in hilly countryside and inclement weather needs clarity and consistency in requested behaviours.

Some dogs also are naturally inclined to respond to a whistle. Many gundogs seem predisposed to positive reactions when they hear whistles. This could be a result of early association training as young puppies by proactive breeders, or because it is a clear noise that can be quickly and easily paired with a suitable reinforcer. It is equally possible to accidentally make a dog fearful of whistle noise if care is not taken during first exposure. If your dog is already sensitive to sounds, as well as getting a full health check (noise sensitivity is closely linked to pain), take care to introduce whistle work carefully and gradually.

The whistle signals work

There is another very simple reason that I like using a whistle in my training toolkit. When I pop my whistle lanyard over my head, it is a clear signal to my spaniels that we are heading out for work, walk or play. They know what to expect. When I lift the whistle to my mouth, it is a further visual cue to my team that the serious stuff starts now. In the same way as they recognise certain clothes and equipment mean we are about to do specific activities, the whistle is a clear indication of what we are about to do and what some of the expectations will be. For me, whistles are both functional and fun essentials in my dog training kit.

ADDING A WHISTLE TO YOUR TRAINING TOOLBOX

The first thing you need to do if you would like to start using a whistle is to choose what will be most suitable for you and your dog.

Choosing a whistle

There are a number of options that you can explore, ranging from very attractive hand-carved horn or antler whistles to the plastic gundog whistle. There are also the shepherds' whistles, which are held between the teeth, and metal 'silent' whistles that are designed to have a pitch of noise audible to dogs, but inaudible to people. These whistles are adjusted in pitch and tone by screwing the parts together to a specific position. Occasionally, people choose to use a referee's whistle in metal or plastic, usually as a defined recall whistle. These are all potential options but can have some drawbacks.

The shepherd's whistle can take a lot of practice to get right and is not always the easiest for everyday use out walking. Referees' whistles can be excessively loud and are not conducive to good neighbourly relations if you are blowing it repeatedly in the park early in the morning or late at night.

Silent whistles are preferred by many handlers and field triallers but can be a little more difficult for novice handlers to become confident with. Sometimes, there is a lack of awareness of whether the whistle has actually been sounded, depending on the pitch the whistle has been adjusted to. I have known these whistles to sometimes unscrew slightly, altering the sound, which affects consistency. It is also possible for them to unscrew fully, losing one part, usually never to be found again, and rendering the whistle useless. Invariably, this always happens at the least ideal moment and when you need your whistle more than ever.

A selection of plastic gundog whistles typically used for spaniels.

Gundog whistles

While there is a wide range of whistle options, a plastic gundog whistle is a solid choice. This is for consistency, ease of use, convenience and they have several advantages over other options. One significant disadvantage of individually carved or manufactured whistles is that they can be very distinct in their pitch, tone and overall sound. If you lose your whistle, you might need to retrain your dog to recognise a new one.

Plastic gundog whistles have a consistent pitch and have identifying numbers, meaning it is easy to replace lost or broken ones with another. This aids consistency, as your dog will become familiar with not only how you blow your whistle and your individual cues, but also the pitch and tone of your whistle. There are certain traditions relating to the use of specific whistle numbers with certain breeds and functions of gundogs, notably whether they are likely to work close

Have spare whistles in different places in case you lose or forget one.

to you or at a distance. In truth, it is more important that you are consistent with your choice of whistle. Keep a note of your chosen whistle number in case you ever need to replace it – this can be found printed on the underside of your whistle and also on the original packaging when purchased.

One common question is how your dog will know it is your whistle if other handlers close by are using the same whistle pitch. Do not worry. Even if every other handler is using the same whistle as you, everyone will have their own individual way of blowing the whistle, which will include subtle differences in the cues used. With practice, our dogs learn to recognise their own whistle and whistle cues.

It is recommended that you buy at least two identical whistles with the same pitch and keep them in different places – perhaps one in the car, another on your keys, one on a lanyard or in your coat pocket. This means you will hopefully always have one to hand and a spare if you lose or forget one.

These whistles are also inexpensive, very robust and long-lasting (I have several that are well over twenty years old now) and are easily cleaned by washing with warm water and detergent. Some people will pop them in their dishwasher. Other handlers choose to clean their whistles by immersing them in a chosen alcoholic beverage for a short time!

Finally, these whistles come in a range of colours if style, fashion and outfit matching is important to you. Choose a suitable lanyard to attach your whistle and hang round your neck. That way your whistle is always easy to access, and you do not find yourself fumbling in pockets trying to find it as you watch your spaniel disappear over the horizon.

INTRODUCING THE WHISTLE

Be wary of rushing into using your whistle before you and your dog have become familiar with it and its sounds. Like everything else, your dog needs to learn what the whistle means and what the expectations are. It is also important that you become comfortable and familiar with using the whistle. It becomes an integral part of working your spaniel. On a day working or field training my team, my whistle will spend more time in my mouth than hanging around my neck because I need it there for instant use and responses. This needs practice to become second nature to you and your spaniel.

First steps

The first thing to practise is putting the whistle in your mouth, lightly holding it between your teeth and practise saying some of your verbal cue words. Your dog's name is a good one to practise, as well as other basic cues such as 'sit' or 'come'. Do this first without your dog to avoid confusion. You also need to practise being able to speak while holding the whistle in your mouth, without accidentally blowing the whistle or drooling everywhere. This will help you learn to control how you hold the whistle and also help you start training your dog to link new whistle cues to existing verbal cues.

Being able to hold the whistle in your mouth and talk is also useful preparation for situations in which you might urgently need to use it. Rarely do you have time to find your whistle, pop it into your mouth and blow your cue. By that time, your spaniel might be half a field (or further) away from you. Your whistle needs to be readily accessible and ready to use, especially in urgent or emergency situations.

Build a positive whistle association

Once you are confident at popping the whistle in your mouth and being able to control it, start introducing your dog to the presence and movement of the whistle. I like to create a positive association of the whistle moving to my mouth for my dog so that they learn the whistle is a signal of things about to happen and behavioural expectations.

I do this even before starting to make whistle sounds. Simply take some tasty food rewards and each time you lift the whistle to your mouth and pop it between your teeth, drop or throw a food reward to your dog. This can help to create a positive association with the whistle for your spaniel, even before you start to make whistle sounds and the movement of the whistle to your mouth can signal that attention to you is required.

USING THE WHISTLE

It sounds like overkill, but practising using your whistle before expecting your spaniel to respond to it is important. You do need to be able to be consistent in how you blow your whistle and the specific cues you decide to use. The mechanics of using your whistle are also important: being able to hold it in your mouth ready for use; between your teeth while you also give verbal cues; and just being able to hold the whistle in your mouth for long periods of time.

Practice makes perfect

Practise blowing your whistle and become familiar with how to make your desired sounds, as well as how to change the intensity of the sound made. Do this without your spaniel. Once you are confident that you can use your whistle consistently and clearly, and you feel comfortable using it, then you can start introducing your dog to the sound of the whistle and build a positive association with the sound and behavioural expectations.

If your spaniel already has solid and consistent responses to verbal cues, you can introduce your whistle cue with your verbal cue, mark, and then reward appropriately. This way you can expand your training repertoire broadly and rapidly. Do this in a structured way to help your dog transition from verbal cue to whistle cue.

First, with your whistle in your mouth, say your verbal cue then immediately follow it with your whistle cue, mark and reward the desired behaviour. You can also incorporate body language or hand signals too. This will help your dog succeed and aid the generalisation of the behaviour to the new whistle cues.

Repeat and rehearse in a range of situations to proof the behaviour and gradually fade out alternative and supportive cues (voice and/or body language) until your dog can perform the desired behaviour on the whistle cue alone. Practice will make perfect, or as close to perfect as possible! Do not forget to continue to practise your verbal and body language cues separately too – they will always be useful in different situations and can be a safety net option should your spaniel not respond to a whistle cue.

If whistles are a worry

Whistle sounds can worry some dogs, so always start with gentle introductions to the sound of your whistle, just in case. Avoid blowing your whistle very loudly initially. Instead, consider starting to sound it gently at your dog's mealtimes or at other times when your dog is relaxed, and the whistle sound can be linked to other nice experiences. This helps set your spaniel up for success and creates a favourable link between whistle and enjoyable situations without pressure or expectations. This might be especially important when introducing the whistle to older dogs or those who are sound-sensitive.

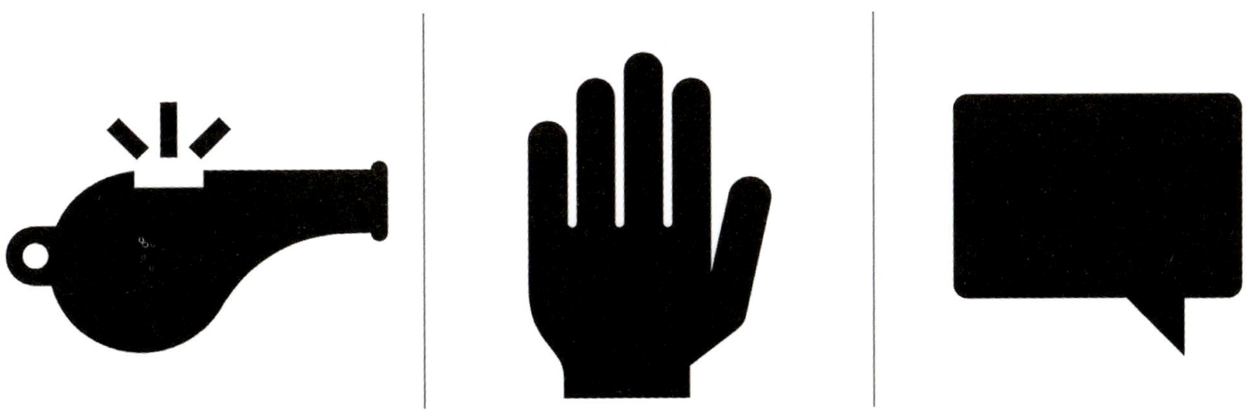

Whistle cues can be used alongside verbal and body language cues.

Whistle training is an effective way to communicate with your spaniel and help gain their attention and focus.

Build a positive association to the whistle sound

You want your spaniel to know the sound of the whistle is a good thing and a predictor of rewards. The easiest way to do this is to link access to nice things to the whistle sound. This can be done with food, toys or other rewards – anything your dog enjoys and finds reinforcing, although a thrown food reward timed with the whistle noise is often an easy way to start.

You can then start training specific behaviours to whistle cues. In order to perfect solid and consistent responses to the whistle, lots of practice, lots of repetition and lots of rewarding is essential.

THE WHISTLE CUES

You can put any behaviour on a whistle cue. Your only limitation will be the variety and complexity of the whistle sounds you can make, plus your training imagination.

There are, however, some typical behaviours that are trained to whistle cues and most relate to gundog work requirements. What will work for you and your spaniel really depends on your own situation, requirements and ambitions. At the very least, having recall on a whistle cue can be infinitely useful and a fantastic emergency 'back up' if it is ever needed. Some handlers will only ever train recall to the whistle and never use their whistle for anything else. Other handlers will train a variety of behaviours to the whistle.

You also have flexibility in determining what whistle sounds you make for the behaviours you want to capture on a whistle cue. There are some standard ones, but many trainers and handlers have their own ideas and reasons for individual variations.

What follows is not a prescriptive list of cues and expectations. Feel free to amend and evolve to suit your own situation, but make sure you are clear on expectations from your spaniel and consistent in how you ask. It is also useful to keep a written record of your own cues and expectations (alongside details of your whistles).

Attention

I train an 'attention' whistle cue, which is very much a 'check-in' and test to see that my dog can respond to me. It can be a useful 'warm up' training exercise. It is effectively the reflex-to-name exercise, but on a whistle cue, and I tend to use it as an initial check for a response in a novel environment or in a situation where I want to know my spaniel is 'with me' rather than engaged in the environment. This can also be a really useful way to introduce the whistle sound to your dog with an easy to identify and reward outcome. It is the first whistle exercise I train to older dogs and introduce in classes.

- *The cue* – a very short, light, single 'pip' on the whistle.
- *The sound* – 'pip'.
- *The expectation* – the dog orients to handler and makes eye contact. This is not a turn or recall whistle and the orientation can be at a distance or in close proximity. Over time and especially with a hard-hunting spaniel in the field, the single pip can become a turn whistle, and you might hear trainers and field triallers use it in this way. For an experienced dog, the single, short whistle pip becomes a little 'nudge' or 'hello you!' to encourage a specific hunting and turning pattern.
- *How to train it* – the attention whistle can be trained in exactly the same way as the reflex to name cue. This can be easily done by linking your dog's name verbally with a short pip on the whistle. When you get orientation to you and eye contact, reward and reinforce it by marking the behaviour, followed by food or toy reward delivery. Start off by linking the verbal cue with the whistle cue, then gradually fade out the name so the single whistle pip also results in orientation and eye contact. An important aspect to this cue is that you reward the dog where they are when they respond to you – this might mean throwing a food or toy reward to them if they are at a distance. This is not a recall whistle, so you do not want to reward your dog returning to you. In some situations, you will use this cue as a way of connecting with your spaniel at distance and asking them to undertake another behaviour, such as finding a retrieve item.

The 'attention' whistle is a way to check connection with your spaniel.

Recall

Recall is an essential skill for any dog to have. It is a behaviour that can keep your dog safe and is a fundamental life skill for your spaniel. You need to have the ability to recall your dog back to you in every situation and over long and short distances. Using a whistle can really support and enhance your everyday recall or for recalling in specific situations such as gundog work or events.

Recall is a skill to which you should devote lots of positive and high-reward training time. If your spaniel knows that returning to you is going to result in nice, fun things, then they are more and more likely to do so, even in the face of distractions, temptations and potential external rewards such as scents, other dogs, people and wildlife. No dog has a 100 per cent recall – they are living, sentient beings just like us – but you should certainly aim for 99.9 per cent and a solid whistle recall can help ensure this.

- *The cue* – can vary but a whistle recall is typically multiple 'peeps', sometimes with a tune. My own recall cue mimics the verbal cue I use with very young puppies to encourage them to come towards me – 'pup, pup, pup, pup'. During training, I like to repeat the recall cue until the dog is back within touching distance (and I can attach their lead if needed). They can then be rewarded well for doing so. Some handlers advocate two or three whistle peeps for recall, and this can work well. However, I have found that some dogs, especially if recalling over a longer distance, can lose focus and get distracted. For this reason, I like to use multiple 'peeps' for a solid and consistent recall and certainly in early training to reinforce the behaviour and link it to the whistle cue.
- *The sound* – 'pip pip pip piiiiip, pip pip pip piiiiip'.
- *The expectation* – that when your dog hears the recall cue, they immediately turn towards you/the sound of the whistle and return as fast as possible. They then stay within your close vicinity (and certainly close enough to have their lead attached if necessary) until permitted to do something else.
- *How to train it* – the recall whistle cue can be trained informally and in more formal ways. A great way to introduce it is at mealtimes, ideally when your dog is in a different room from their meal being prepared. Call them to come for their meal and blow your recall whistle cue at the same time. When they arrive, provide their food and stop blowing the recall whistle. This is a fabulous way to condition a great response easily

The recall whistle is an essential cue.

and reliably to the recall whistle. More formal recall whistle training will involve sounding your recall whistle while doing 'puppy recalls' with your spaniel on and off lead/long line and recalling over longer distances when your dog is pottering around as well as when you have asked them to wait in a specific position and place. The key to a reliable and consistent recall is to rehearse success frequently and reward and reinforce heavily. Avoid recall failure – always set your spaniel up to succeed and do not use your recall whistle in early training unless you know you can reinforce the behaviour. This is one reason I like the 'attention' whistle as a sort of safety net. If I blow the attention cue and get zero response, then I am not going to get a recall response either. You can also avoid any failure in early training by using a long line to keep some connection with your spaniel and to permit reinforcement of recall if necessary.

Stop

The stop whistle is used when you need your spaniel to stop, instantly – and stay in position until the next behaviour is requested. The stop whistle might be used if your spaniel starts to chase something, you need to stop them to redirect them or in an emergency situation when you need them to stop any further movement for their safety.

- *The cue* – a long, single blast, often backed up by a police-style raised arm and hand visible cue. In training, this can also be backed up with a verbal cue such as 'STOP'.
- *The sound* – 'peeeeeeeeeeeeep!'.
- The expectation – your spaniel should stop as quickly as possible and wait in that location and position until you ask them to do something else – recall, retrieve or to carry on. The stop is often a default 'sit' with the thinking that if your dog is sitting, then they are less likely to move. A sit can also be useful in some situations where your dog might be expected to stay there for a prolonged period at a distance from you. I have seen dogs in tests, trials and in the working environment have to sit and wait for more than ten minutes while another dog undertakes a retrieve. Being able to stay still in one place and be steady is essential – a sit can help make this easy and is a consistent behaviour, which can also aid training the behaviour. However, for some dogs, asking for and enforcing a sit can be difficult, especially if they find it uncomfortable. You might decide that a stop in a standing position is acceptable, or even a down. The disadvantage of a down might be that your dog struggles to see you, especially in cover or long grass, so often a sit or stand is preferred.
- *How to train it* – a stop can be trained by asking for a sit/stand/stay verbally close to you and blowing the stop whistle cue. Mark and reward. This can be

The stop whistle indicates that your dog should stop and remain still.

a good way to make the expected behaviour clear to your dog. Alternatively, walk with your dog at your side and blow the stop whistle while asking them to stop/sit and reward desired behaviour. As the stop behaviour becomes robust and consistent, you can start to add movement away from and around your dog while they remain still. A solid stop can also be captured by allowing your spaniel to hunt around close to you and as they turn towards you, step towards them, blow the stop whistle and combine with a clear hand signal and suitable verbal cue. To reward a stop, the ability to throw a food reward or even a toy over your dog's head will encourage your dog to not only stop, but to also remain at a distance from you and get a valued reward for doing so.

Turn

The turn whistle is useful as an indication to make a 180-degree turn and then continue moving. This might be when working a hunt pattern and you need your spaniel to turn back towards you. Alternatively, your spaniel could be starting to range a little further than ideal. Out walking, you might be choosing a different path to your spaniel and the turn whistle can say 'this way please!'.

The turn whistle should result in a fluid turn back towards you.

The turn cue is not a recall or a stop. It is intended to result in a fluid turn movement that allows your spaniel to make turns in a direction desired and managed by their handler but with flow and momentum and sometimes at a distance from their handler. It is supported by clear body language cues from the handler in the form of hand, shoulder, leg and feet cues to indicate the desired plane of movement.

- *The cue* – a double 'peep-peep', which might also be accompanied by the handler changing their body movement to further encourage the dog to turn towards them.
- *The sound* – 'pip pip'.
- *The expectation* – upon hearing the turn whistle, your spaniel stops further forwards movement, makes a 180-degree turn and continues to move in the new direction, ideally while also making a micro or more sustained 'check-in' with you.
- *How to train it* – the turn whistle cue can be trained by capturing the in-built hunting and quartering behaviour that is inherent in many spaniels or by more mechanical training methods. If you are capturing the turn, simply allow your spaniel to hunt some ground, ideally ground with scent. Most spaniels will start to move in a zig zag motion, and you can time and link your turn whistle cue with them making a turn towards you. If a turn is successful, you can reward by allowing them to continue to hunt or throw a food/toy reward in the new direction to encourage that forward movement. For an older dog who might be less inclined to demonstrate that behaviour, or in a situation where the training ground is not very interesting, you can work on the turn whistle using food rewards/lures. Start with your dog facing you and some food in both hands. Throw a piece of food (large enough that your dog can see and smell it easily!) about two metres to your side – if throwing it to your left, throw with your right hand and orient your body in that direction and vice versa. Your dog should head out to get the reward and as they eat it, blow your turn 'pip pip', reorient your body in the opposite direction and throw another food reward. The aim is your dog moving in a fluid zig zag fashion in front of you, covering ground

while you move in a straight line forward, but supporting your dog in turning with whistle and body language cues.

Hunt

The desire and drive to hunt is embedded in spaniel DNA. It is an essential skill for working spaniels to have. In gundog tests and trials, hunting should be stylish and functional and for working gundogs, being able to hunt is key to their roles in the field.

The hunt whistle is a behaviour more commonly trained in retrieving breeds such as Labradors. It is used to indicate where the dog should start looking for an item that needs to be found and retrieved, especially at a distance from their handler. It can also be useful for our spaniels, who might need help in locating an item at a distance, or to encourage hunting and 'holding' within a specific area – again, usually to find something to be retrieved.

- The cue – a 'twit twoo' or a 'twoo twit', which sounds a little like an owl hooting. The 'twoo twit' version can be useful for dogs who might respond to the initial, short 'twit' in 'twit twoo' by looking at their handler, rather than starting to hunt.
- The expectation – the hunt whistle is your spaniel's cue to get their nose to the ground in their immediate area and hunt – that is, to sniff and search. They might be looking for a retrieve item that needs to be recovered, a lost bird if they are working, or even your lost car keys! This is often a really fun and very functional whistle cue to teach your spaniel.
- How to train it – the easiest way I have found to train the hunt whistle is to simply blow it when your spaniel is already busy sniffing an area. If they stop sniffing, stop blowing the whistle. You can also scatter some small food rewards on the ground and allow your spaniel to search for them, all the time blowing the hunt whistle. When all the treats have been found and eaten, stop blowing the whistle and reset to start again.

The hunt whistle is a way to communicate to your spaniel to start searching for something – often an item to be retrieved.

If you are consistent, clear, mark and then reward your desired behaviour with your whistle cue well, you will very quickly have a responsive spaniel. Your whistle might just become an essential part of your spaniel training toolkit and your everyday spaniel walking attire.

TOP TIPS FOR WHISTLING WHILE YOU WORK

- A whistle is a useful part of your spaniel walking and training kit, making communication clear and consistent.
- Choose a whistle that is consistent, and you can replace easily – they have a surprising knack for getting lost and misplaced!
- Plastic, gundog whistles are available in consistent pitches so are easy to replace, cost effective, and also come in a range of colours to match your outfits.
- Practise using your whistle and holding it between your teeth before using with your spaniel.
- Your whistle should be ready in your mouth in situations where you might need to use it – if it is hanging around your neck, by the time you have found it and got it to your mouth, your spaniel could be long gone.
- Whistle cues can be used for a range of different behaviours – be as creative as you wish, as long as you are being consistent with cues and expectations.

CHAPTER 7

REALLY GOOD RECALL

When you ask, does your spaniel come back to you? Do they return with gusto and speed 100 per cent of the time, or does it depend on: where you are; how far away they are; what smells there are; if there are other dogs around; or a myriad of other reasons why they might not be back beside you as fast as possible?

'COME BACK!' – RECALL, A SPECIFIC LIFE SKILL

Recall is one of the most common concerns that spaniel caregivers report issues with. People often describe their spaniel as being 'good as gold' until a scent or movement (often birds or other wildlife) distracts them.

Does your recall look like this? Running past and ignoring you?

The reliable recall you thought you had from training classes and as seen in your sitting room, garden and maybe even your usual dog walk, vanishes – almost as fast as your spaniel has.

The frustrating thing is that during puppyhood and early adolescence, spaniels typically stick close to their person – sometimes too close! This can lead to a false sense of security that their recall is great and the likelihood of them straying is low. We reduce the level of reinforcement that we might once have been using and become complacent.

Almost overnight, that limpet-like spaniel becomes a whirling dervish who vanishes in a nanosecond, chasing a smell, a leaf, a dog or something else that has taken their fancy. This typically happens as adolescence hits, around five to eight months old – a result of increased confidence and biological changes.

This has happened to 99.9 per cent of anyone who has ever walked a dog. Dogs are sentient beings who get tired, excited, distracted, frustrated and have situations where their ability to resist temptation is sorely tested. The problem is that sometimes, this tests our relationship with them, too. Even the best trained and consistent spaniel will have 'off days' and no recall or close proximity behaviour is 100 per cent. I advise my own coaching clients that we should aim for 99 per cent recall – they should return with little or no hesitation. When the one per cent 'blip' does happen – perhaps a slow return or no immediate appearance despite calling or whistling, this is an opportunity to reset, remind and heavily reward our spaniel about what recall, and maintenance of proximity behaviour means.

THE SPANIEL THRILL-SEEKER AND DOPAMINE CHASER

Spaniels are the ultimate thrill-seekers, almost constantly looking for their next dopamine hit.

All spaniels have off days thanks to distractions and temptations.

Sometimes recall means an end to fun times for our spaniels.

Recall is important so that you can call your spaniel off interesting situations and distractions.

Searching for it can become intensely self-rewarding. As a result, your once perfect recall no longer works. You might have no response at all and be left watching your spaniel have an absolute ball in front of you (or disappearing over the horizon) while almost studiously 'ignoring' you. They might have learned that recalling means an end to the fun they were having, so you have a spaniel who comes to almost touching distance and then dances away as you try to reattach the lead.

The transition from puppy to adolescent and then to adulthood are stages where we want to ramp up recall reinforcement and reward our spaniels like they have won the lottery when they recall whether it is a simple return back into the house, or recalling off the temptation of a bird, rabbit, person, other dog, cat or any other potentially interesting distraction. These are also the stages where we see behavioural regression (often hormone related) so understanding and preparation that you might need to take some steps back in your training is essential.

Whatever recall concern you are having, you are not alone. Recall is a skill that needs constant practice, rehearsal in a range of situations and lots of reinforcement and reward. As well as recall, teaching your spaniel 'proximity' behaviour is also essential and as a default behaviour, is an important foundation to your recall needs.

WHY RECALL IS IMPORTANT

A recall is an essential skill for anyone with a dog. Recall keeps your spaniel safe and under control. If you do not have a solid and consistent recall, then your spaniel should be on a lead or long line. The risk of harm is just too great. In many locations, there are local regulations and requirements for dogs to be on lead (or under 'close control') and if you are in the vicinity of livestock then it is essential.

We have a social and legal responsibility to keep our dogs under close control. This could be off lead, running free (in suitable places and spaces) or in a more managed way using leads or long lines. Off-lead freedom might seem like a 'must have' for our dogs – especially highly active spaniels who are delighted when free running – but it is also a privilege and one that must be earned.

To let any dog who does not have a reliable recall or consistent maintenance of close proximity to you off lead to run free in an unmanaged and uncontrolled environment (and potentially cause havoc) is downright irresponsible. It is also potentially dangerous for the dog, yourself and even other animals and people. I have heard people say 'ah but they always come back, eventually' sometimes followed by a quiet confession that their dog has effectively been lost for several hours before finding their way home. The terrifying thing is that in the time that any dog is not under close supervision, there is the risk of them coming across unfriendly dogs or people, wildlife, livestock (and the seriousness of the potential consequences of that cannot be overestimated), roads, railway lines or a host of other dangers.

If our spaniel does disappear, we must make a concerted effort not to let it happen again. For consistent re-offenders, it is important to recognise that every time they run free and likely have an amazing, highly rewarding time, we are effectively training them to do exactly that.

Instead, we must learn from it and use it as a clear sign that our training, rehearsing consistent and reliable recall, and maintaining proximity behaviour needs to be more solidly applied. We need our spaniels to be in the habit of keeping close, checking in, being aware of where we each are, managing their own speed and returning to us when asked.

A good recall means that you can help to keep your dog safe and also help to keep other people and their pets safe too – remember that not everyone likes dogs and indeed, not every dog likes other dogs. Just because your dog is friendly, it is not fair to assume that every other dog will be, nor is it fair to allow your dog to approach other dogs without express permission, and especially if you cannot recall your dog away. Dogs that approach other dogs with their caregiver shouting behind them 'it's ok, they are friendly' are

Teaching proximity behaviour is a good foundation for keeping your spaniel close to you, so that extensive recalls are not necessary.

dogs with very poor social skills and are actually not being 'friendly'. Imagine if you were out walking, minding your own business and an unknown person ran up to you and gave you a hug. I suspect you would be less than impressed and would certainly not identify the person responsible as 'friendly' or harmless.

A good recall also means that you can get your dog away from potential danger or anything that could be a potential hazard. It is an essential life skill that should be one of the most basic behaviours that our spaniels learn. It is also a skill that must be able to be performed in a range of situations of high and low distraction.

Finally, a good recall is also an important part of a range of canine activities and dog sports. If you fancy working towards training awards, or taking part in competitive disciplines, recall is an integral part of those.

A really good recall is critical.

THE 'SPANIEL SPORTS CAR'

The spaniel ability to go from zero to sixty miles an hour faster than a Formula 1 car means that a solid recall is essential. One second they are right beside us, but very quickly, they can be three fields away, heading into the next county. The distance covered at speed also means that there is the potential for them to be beyond typical voice or whistle recall distance surprisingly fast. For this reason (as well as all the obvious safety ones) a rapid reflex to your recall cue is very highly desirable.

However, as an adjunct to a good, rapid and reliable recall, it is also important that your spaniel develops consistent 'proximity' behaviour. Get this right and a lot of recall issues vanish.

Training a really good recall is vital.

THE 'CIRCLE OF TRUST', OR PROXIMITY BEHAVOUR

There is an argument that while recall is an important skill for your dog to have, if they are always in your close vicinity, then recall is largely not needed. In effect they learn to stay within close proximity to your position and if they realise they have strayed outside of the desired proximity, then they will self-'correct'. Think of this behaviour as an imaginary long line, that when your spaniel is nearing the end of, they stop and either wait or return to you.

Many working spaniels demonstrate this behaviour, and it is something I actively work on much more now with my spaniels than I may have initially done. It is about creating an invisible 'boundary' that your off-lead spaniel stays within. They are then unlikely to disappear over the horizon, or if they do look like they are about to accelerate away, they are close enough that you should be able to respond to the situation.

Within my little team of spaniels, that boundary size is very individual. For my mature, experienced team members, the boundary is easily around five metres and, in some situations, it will be larger. If they wander beyond that distance from me, I ask them to come back towards me – it might be a full recall, it might just be a 'wait there' with me catching up. For my more inexperienced team members, the circle of trust is much smaller, and if there have been some recent 'recall blips', I might be expecting them to be holding a position at my side.

The boundary is also dynamic depending on the external situation and circumstances. For example, walking in a new location that we are unsure of, the circle is very tight, and I expect close proximity to be maintained – probably on lead initially. If there are lots of people, dogs, potential wildlife (look for the signs of this – droppings, earth scrapes, scents or visual identification) or it is clear that there is a lot of scent on the ground, I have similar expectations. In a more sterile environment, I might be a little more relaxed BUT: a word of caution here. If your spaniel is a 'seeker' and is likely to want to search for their dopamine-fuelled pleasure hit, a sterile environment can sometimes mean they are more likely to push those boundaries in an effort to find their reward. Also be aware that many spaniels actively seek boundaries such as hedges to explore and hunt, so these landmarks can become hugely tempting.

Maintaining proximity is important even for working spaniels.

Teaching proximity behaviour

To teach and reinforce an effective 'circle of trust' starts from day one with your puppy. If you have an older rehomed dog or want to start this work afresh with your dog (of any age but remember that for an older dog with a reinforcement history of poor recall and environmental rewards, this will take longer), the same principles apply.

Encourage your spaniel to stay with you. Find an open space with minimal distractions, have lots of small, tasty treats, or a tug toy if preferred and just start moving around – wander. Small puppies can usually be off lead for this exercise, an older dog might be better on a trailing long line, so that you can manage any blips. Every time your dog turns towards you and comes within your desired proximity distance (hint – I would suggest rewarding as close to you as possible always) drop some treats onto the ground at your feet. Then move away, keeping an eye on them finishing the treats and look for a head lift. As the head lifts and they move towards you (no cues here) drop some more treats at your feet. Repeat this exercise lots – I still do this even with my really experienced and recall-savvy spaniels as a little reminder and also as a fun exercise that says, 'my feet are predictors of nice stuff – it's good to keep an eye on where they are!'

THE RECALL CUE

For a reliable, really good recall, you will need a defined recall cue. I have several cues all linked to recall but have different expectations. Identify what works best for you. If you have already been using a recall cue (verbal or whistle) that is not working, it could have become toxic. This means that your spaniel no longer has any positive association with it and no matter how often you use it, they are not going to reliably recall to it. In this case, find an alternative and start again.

Recall cues can also be multiple. In early recall training I crouch down, arms open and welcoming and use voice and whistle cues as well as body language. This develops a response to all three cues, but also practise using each cue individually too – this helps to ensure a consistent response.

The location of your feet can reward proximity behaviour.

Recall needs to be good, even just to be able to play with your spaniel.

EXAMPLES OF VERSIONS OF RECALL CUES AND EXPECTATIONS

COME – please return to me now (must return to touching distance, close enough to put lead on/hold) – multiple peeps on the whistle means the same thing and can be used with the verbal cue.

PUP PUP PUP – this is a loose recall cue that I use with all small puppies, and I pair with mealtimes. All my adult dogs still respond to this, and it is a less formal recall than 'come' so will often be used when out walking, more for attention, partial recalls and keeping my spaniels semi-close. I use this cue in the garden when we are relaxed but perhaps a spaniel is investigating something I would rather they did not.

TOO FAR – not really a recall, but a cue which means you have moved too far outside the 'circle of trust' so please slow down/wait/there/orient back towards me. When I say 'free', you can continue.

'COOKIES' – rarely used in daily life (possibly for obvious reasons!) but this is my emergency recall cue, which has been trained and paired with AMAZING rewards. Only used in an extreme situation, but is regularly topped up with training.

Think about your needs and expectations and identify some cues that might be useful for your spaniel's recall and proximity behaviour.

Practise recall on every walk and in lots of different places.

THE PUPPY RECALL

Puppy recall is one of the most basic recall exercises and it is useful even with adult dogs. You can do it on or off lead (if off lead, work in a controlled, low-distraction environment initially). Start by taking a few steps forward with your puppy at your side – you might have a food lure in the hand closest to your puppy at their nose. Then slow and start to take a few steps backwards and take the food lure to your front, meaning your puppy follows your hand and is now in front of you. Move backwards, saying their name and your recall cue. Reward in front of you after a few steps. Repeat – LOTS. In a little puppy walk or play session, you can easily rehearse this simple recall exercise several times.

I still throw in puppy recalls with my older dogs too, just to reinforce the value of coming in close to my front and that 'come' means come back to me, no matter what they are doing or where they are.

THE 'VILLAGE HALL' RECALL

If you have been to dog training classes in the local village hall, you might have practised recall by leaving your dog in a wait (or the trainer holds your dog), walking away from them to a set distance, turning to face them, recalling them and asking for a sit in front of you. This mimics competitive obedience exercises. I still train and teach this, but as an additional recall exercise, alongside all the other situations in which I ask for a recall.

The problem with the 'village hall' recall is that it does not teach a general recall. If your spaniel is ambling along in front of you, sniffing and thinking about other things, this exercise does not really meet the needs of a 'reality recall', so while it can absolutely help your spaniel's overall learning, do not rely on this exercise for training a really good recall.

THE REALITY RECALL

The reality recall is one where your spaniel is likely off lead, pottering along sniffing and enjoying themselves. You then realise that there is something (a person, dog, runner, bike, anything) that you need to have some control of your spaniel around, so you recall them.

Your spaniel needs to be able to disengage with what they are doing, orient and return to you, ideally as fast as possible and then be managed, whether that is lead on or something else.

You can start training a reality recall with your puppy from Day One of them being home. Every time you feed them, call them and add your desired recall cue. If they are pottering about on the floor beside you, get down beside them and call them, making coming to you great fun. Progress to letting them have a sniff in the garden, move a few steps and recall. Do this with mature dogs too, especially if you need to re-address recall. Every time your spaniel comes to you, reward, fuss them and make recalling a great choice.

I then progress to dropping a handful of treats on the ground, letting my dog start to eat them and then run away a few steps. The timing is crucial here – look for your puppy/dog get near to finishing the treats OR if they notice you moving and look up, call them.

Do not forget to tell your spaniel they are brilliant, especially on a difficult recall.

This little exercise starts to build the pattern that you can be sniffing or involved in something really interesting, but if you recall to me, something equally good or even better happens.

In daily life, too, every time your spaniel recalls away from something that you think 'wow!', tell them they are the best dog in the world. Practice makes perfect and the more we rehearse really good recall, the better it will be, even in the face of temptations.

WHEN RECALL GOES WRONG – WHAT TO DO

Our spaniels are not robots. They make mistakes. Sometimes they do not hear us or are tired. Sometimes the world around them is just too exciting and interesting and their previously solid recall gets a little ropey. Sometimes we have inadvertently let things slip a little, too – you know, instead of your spaniel returning promptly to you on the first verbal or whistle cue, you have had to start repeating it and perhaps even subtly changing the cue they are responding to:

Our spaniels are not robots – they make mistakes, including on recall.

'Spot come!' Spot does not recall. 'Spot COME.' Spot does not recall. 'SPOT COME HERE NOW!.'

Spot recalls – but on the different tone and different cue.

No dog ever has 100 per cent recall, but if you are getting a solid recall 99 per cent of the time, that really is excellent. What should you do when it fails though? Your spaniel does not respond either to verbal or whistle cues and is either busy doing their own thing in front of you, disappearing into the distance, or even worse, has already vanished.

Why has your recall gone really bad?

If recall has become sloppy, a little reflection as to why is a good idea. Have things become vague for your dog? Has recall rewarding reduced significantly, making NOT recalling more rewarding? Has there been an incident that made recalling a low priority to your spaniel – a super-exciting time was had playing/hunting/chasing? Are there seasonal changes that are making scents and smells much more interesting? There is a myriad of reasons as to why recall can become less robust. Most of them have absolutely nothing to do with your spaniel 'ignoring' you deliberately or 'trying you on' and are about how they are responding to their environment at a given point in time.

Remember that our dogs do what they find rewarding and for what there has been a history of being rewarded for. If recalling to you has been rewarding (and remains so), you will have increased the likelihood of that behaviour being repeated. If, on the other hand, free running, self-hunting and NOT remaining close to you or recalling rapidly has been rewarded (usually accidentally), then it is likely that behaviour will be repeated. It is essential to remember this if you are working on (or re-working on) recall. You need to re-balance the source of the reinforcement and reward – is it coming from you or the environment? – and increase your spaniel's motivation for returning to you when recalled.

When recall goes wrong – the emergency responses

When recall fails there are a few options to implement. You often need to think quickly, so having previously thought about the options can help you make a snap decision in the instant to keep you all safe. What follows is about managing a situation rather than training.

Run after them – If a recall cue is not responded to but your spaniel is still within a reasonable distance, running after them is an option. I have certainly done this (nicely!) and found it effective for some dogs as a way of reminding them I exist. At the first sign of movement in the opposite direction to the desired recall, I will repeat the cue and start moving towards them. In many cases this works well and, as soon as you get a reconnection from your spaniel, reward (and probably pop the lead on while you catch your breath, and your heart rate returns to normal). Note that for some dogs this is a definite 'no' and will actually push your spaniel away from you – it is worth knowing your dog and how they will respond to you chasing them.

Stand still – This is useful for a spaniel who might get disoriented on a failed recall and when they do remember to return, they can see you. This is an option in a controlled environment such as an enclosed field or garden, where you can effectively wait quietly until they return. Put the lead on and make a mental note that recall training needs much more practice. Standing still in a park full or people, dogs, wildlife or near livestock or other hazards is not an option – you will need to be more active in trying to get your spaniel back quickly.

Hide – Hiding is a great option both in training and also for temporary 'failed' recalls – the ones where they initially do not respond but you can see them thinking about it. At that point, repeat your recall cue and hide, but somewhere they can still find you – behind a tree or bush. For needy spaniels, this can help remind them of your existence and put the emphasis on them being aware of your location. It can also become a fun game and really increase your dog's desire to recall and find you.

FREEDOM FIELDS AND SECURE DOG PARKS

Secure fields that can be booked on an individual basis for exercising dogs have become incredibly popular. These are facilities that are fully enclosed, secure and are perfect places for your spaniel to have lots of fun and running without you having to worry about them disappearing over the horizon or coming across unexpected dogs, people, wildlife or livestock. They also make great places for a meet up with your human friends for a chat and coffee and your dogs can have a good time together, too.

In a chapter about recall training, they deserve a mention. If you routinely use them and allow your spaniel to run free in them, galloping round the boundaries and fence running with frustration that they cannot get out, you are not helping your recall training. You might end up with a tired spaniel, but not one that has learned to interact with you and be aware of you. Also, the more your spaniel rehearses boundary running, the more likely they are to rehearse it beyond the freedom field – around the boundaries and hedges of actual fields.

If you use freedom fields and dog parks, use them wisely and watch what your spaniel is doing. If they are happily running (perhaps with canine friends) and stopping, sniffing and are able to interact with you when asked, perfect. If, however, you arrive, your spaniel leaps out of your vehicle and runs around like a whirlwind with zero interest in where you are or what you are doing, frenetically quartering the ground and patrolling the boundaries, revise how you are using them.

Recall needs to be consistent and that consistency applied and rehearsed everywhere and in as many contexts as possible.

BE A BOOMERANG – A RECALL GAME FOR YOUR SPANIEL

This is a training game that can be done at home or taken to more exciting environments. It helps to build automatic return behaviour, proximity, and encourages your spaniel to be aware of your body movement to build recall behaviour.

Step 1. Have some tasty treats in both hands and let your spaniel know.

Step 2. With your right hand, throw a treat out to your left*– start by throwing it only a short distance out and it helps if your dog can see it land. Your spaniel should then run to get that treat.

Step 3. Repeat several times from left to right, effectively zig zagging but also moving forwards slowly. If you have space, you can start to move around and increase distance. After your dog has run in one direction for the treat, wait to see that they have found it and eaten it and, as their head lifts, throw a treat in the opposite direction, while also turning your feet and shoulders that way. You might even take a few steps in the opposite direction. This encourages your dog to look for you AND to start to follow your body language (or your feet and shoulders – dogs typically follow where our feet go).

Step 4. Once you have an established zig zag pattern and your spaniel is 'being like a boomerang' every now and again, instead of throwing a treat out to the side, call your dog using your recall cue and encourage your dog to face you and come close – a sit is not necessary – we are working on recall and need to reward the **recall**.

Step 5. Repeat lots and reward lots. The more often your spaniel gets rewarded for being around you and watching what you are doing, the more they will want to stay with you. Equally, the more often your reward is a recall, the more likely they are to recall when you REALLY need it.

**You can equally use your left hand to throw to the left and right hand to throw to the right – I used to do this, but then modified it when I realised that by throwing across my body, I was changing the position of my feet and shoulders, and this encouraged my spaniels to turn with my body movement. It also forms foundations for training hunting behaviours and working on quartering with your spaniel.*

VARIATIONS

You can also practise recall from a 'wait' or 'stay' position (but remember this is not always representative of real life), when they are simply out 'mooching' or from a different room in the house. My golden rule when training this exercise is that, if you cannot guarantee your dog will recall, do not use your recall cue because they will learn to ignore it. Use a long line and especially in areas where temptation might be a problem so that you can reinforce the desired behaviour and manage any unwanted behaviours.

An enthusiastic recall is both a joy and a necessity.

TOP TIPS FOR REALLY GOOD RECALL

- Practise, practise and practise. The more practice you do and the more rewards your dog gets for recalling in all situations and in the face of varied distractions and temptations, the better your recall will be when you really need it.
- Reward, reward, reward every recall in early training well – in a ten-minute walk with a puppy, you can easily do many quick, small recall repetitions, on and off lead/long line. Do not forget to throw in the occasional amazing 'jackpot' reward of something super-tasty or exciting, such as their favourite toy.
- Manage situations and environments when you are training – do a risk assessment to consider if there might be temptations or distractions for your spaniel. If so, use your long line or do some close, proximity work initially.
- If you get to a location where you think a free run will be nice and your spaniel sits staring out in the great blue yonder, unable to respond to basic cues such as their name, do not let them off – they are telling you they are past the point of being able to respond if you need/want them to and you are only reinforcing their self-managed free running.
- Avoid simply letting your spaniel off lead or to free run anywhere – get into the habit of some controlled behaviours first – perhaps facing you before you release them or a few steps of heelwork. You might do a small scatter feed as you unclip the lead to keep the excitement and energy low. All of these build the habit that the lead unclipping is not the signal to run free.
- Remember that most working spaniels will rarely go beyond a few metres of their handler unless they are actively hunting (permitted and controlled) or on a retrieve.
- While expansive and extensive free running for fun might look lovely, unless your recall is solid at a distance, be wary. Temptations and distractions are everywhere and can pop up at a second's notice.
- Expect the same behaviours for recall and proximity everywhere – even in secure fields and dog parks – this helps to build habits of your recall expectations.
- If recall goes wrong, do what you need to do to get your spaniel back if the situation is not safe or secure and, when you do get them back, do not tell them off (even if you are stressed and gritting your teeth!). Instead, put them on a lead, count to ten and gently stroke and interact with them, perhaps giving a reward at this point. You want to bring everyone's energy down and reset – do some micro recalls on lead and reward heavily while making a mental note of your next recall training plan, which will likely involve avoiding a repeat of that incident in that location.
- If you are completely stuck and at a loss with recall, seek experienced and professional training help – another set of eyes can often help you see things and work on things you were not aware of, as well as offering alternative perspectives.

CHAPTER 8

HARNESSING THE HUNTER

Spaniels were bred to hunt – it is part of who and what they are. Hunting is something that most spaniels enjoy and find highly rewarding – you just need to watch a spaniel working in the field, nose to the ground, to see how much joy it gives them. We exploit this skill in a range of situations outside traditional gundog work and spaniels can be found 'hunting' for lots of things. Being able to use their nose, brain and body to find, follow and locate the origin of scent is inherently enjoyable for our spaniels and is a fantastic way to exercise their body and mind.

Spaniels love to sniff – that nose was made for sniffing!

For companion spaniels, hunting is not necessarily something they can indulge in frequently. They might be restricted in exercise and their ability to actively find scent and follow it. They might be living and exercising in a relatively scent-sterile urban environment. Alternatively, they might live in a rural environment where there are numerous hunting and scenting opportunities, but none are safe or appropriate. A spaniel in full-on 'sniff mode' can be resistant to normal recall cues or proximity expectations, especially if they have not had the opportunity to practise these skills in the face of good scents and learned focus and self-control (*see* Chapter 5).

Hunting might not just be for scent either. Some spaniels have learned to chase and actively hunt prey by sight. This can become intrinsically rewarding. Prey might be birds, cats, squirrels or rabbits. Working spaniels involved in 'picking up' – the retrieval of shot game – will have come across 'runners'. These are birds that are wounded but not dead. The role of the picking-up dog is to collect them and return them to their handler for humane dispatch – an essential role for working gundogs. These runners usually need chasing, sometimes over significant distances. I know for my own working spaniels, after working on a few runners in any season, their hunting chase drive increases significantly and we typically have to spend time on remedial training as a result. If your spaniel regularly chases local wildlife, then a similar pattern of arousal will develop.

For the non-working spaniel, self-hunting or chasing live prey is not acceptable. We have a responsibility to keep our dogs safe and ensure that they are not interfering with local wildlife, livestock or hunting the neighbourhood cats. It is dangerous and, in many cases, will be illegal. Recognising that it is a real risk with spaniels is important for all caregivers, so that appropriate measures and training can be put in place.

Understanding them as hunting breeds/types helps us work with them to 'harness the hunter'.

A NOSE ON (FAST) LEGS

Dogs have a significant proportion of their brain devoted to scent, its recognition and discrimination. For breeds like spaniels, who have been selectively bred for skills that support hunting, their scenting ability is even further enhanced alongside other physical attributes that make them exceptional hunters.

Spaniels are not only great sniffers, but they are also fast and incredibly athletic too. Your spaniel might be a regular little 'trot along' dog, but in the right circumstances, they can quickly morph into a little speedster and move far faster and more nimbly than we can. They will also be able to get through dense vegetation and into places that we definitely cannot without significant effort. Their four legs also make them much speedier and more able to accelerate than us.

Combine all this with those lovely, decorative ear flaps that sometimes seem to completely occlude their ear canals, apparently preventing any listening, then what we essentially have is a furry nose on very fast legs.

WORKING WITH A HUNTING MACHINE

If you have a hunting machine, you need to learn how to work together. Some spaniels will have more hunting drive than others. This can even be seen in young

Spaniels were bred to hunt – we need to recognise this and harness that skill appropriately.

Our spaniels are noses on very fast legs.

Spaniels have been bred to happily give up their 'prey' to their handlers rather than continuing the predatory sequence to consumption.

puppies before they are weaned – some will instinctively quarter open ground, nose to the floor. Awareness is key and chatting to your spaniel's breeder about their parents and their hunting prowess can be enlightening.

It is always best to work with rather than against hunting. Knowing what hunting looks like is essential and also recognising the point at which there might be no return is also critical for the companion spaniel caregiver. Too often on lost spaniel posts you see the line 'one minute they were trotting along, then their nose went down, and they were gone!'. So, how can you work with your hunting machine?

What does your spaniel's hunting look like?

Identifying when your spaniel is in hunting mode is critical. Hunting follows a series of behaviours described as the predatory sequence, seen in dogs and related species. It starts with identifying potential prey, then sequences through stalking, chasing, grabbing, biting, killing, dissecting and consuming. Different dog breeds have had parts of this behaviour pattern amended as a result of selection – a working gundog who will not happily give up their retrieved 'prey' to their handler is of little value.

However, the general sequence is maintained and is useful in managing your own spaniel's hunting behaviour. Notably, the sequence of predation behaviours progress rapidly and often our dogs are well into the sequence before we have really noticed. This can make interrupting them tricky.

Watch your spaniel carefully when they are out running free (in a safe, enclosed area). Look how they hunt and sniff. Look at their body language. Some spaniels will stop and go quite stiff, staring into the distance looking and sniffing. Others will start to slow down almost stalking scent carefully, and others will become quite animated following the source of scent. Work out what the signs are for your spaniel, because this can help you know when you might want to step in – ideally before the sequence progresses.

Generally, it is the identification or orientation to potential prey that is key in spaniel hunting behaviour, meaning that we need to be alert to that behaviour. We also need to be aware of the environment they are in and the potential for sources of potential prey or hunting interest. This could be old scent, or the presence of potential prey.

Environmental awareness for potential hunting opportunities is essential when training your spaniel.

HOW TO MANAGE YOUR HUNTING MACHINE

A hunting spaniel can be an absolute delight or an utter terror. Even experienced gundog handlers will describe some spaniels as irrepressible hunters and struggle to 'hold' them in a defined area. For the average pet spaniel, the hunting drive to seek out scent or movement can sometimes be overwhelming for their people and can lead to conflict and frustration for dog and handler.

When I have new clients with a hard-hunting spaniel, I always ask what their aim is. If they want to work their spaniel or train them to compete in gundog tests and trials, then whatever hunting pattern they already have will need honing, tidying and often tightening up. I will direct the handlers to suitable trainers who have the facilities, resources and experience to harness these hunting skills in a way that is functional but also manageable for the handler. These dogs need all of their instinctive hunting skills, plus some embellishing to meet the needs of the field or competitive environment.

If your spaniel is to be a companion, then you might be more inclined to look at harnessing their hunting instinct in a more 'pet-friendly' way. By this, I mean hunting for specific items, training hunting games and harnessing their hunting skills and desires in a more fun and less functional way.

Early training and experiences are also critical too. It is essential that we limit the potential for accidental hunting rewards, especially with young dogs. For older spaniels who might have less than desirable hunting behaviours when out exercising, if they are routinely chasing birds, rabbits or squirrels in the garden then do not be surprised when they repeat that behaviour elsewhere. Remember, our spaniels get better at what they rehearse and what they rehearse often becomes highly rewarding.

Embedding other management skills is also important. Check-ins, equipment such as leads and long lines, a reliable and robust recall from distractions and a simple risk assessment are all useful. In any new environment, I always do a mental risk assessment of where we are, where there are roads/tracks/paths/

The working spaniel will need specific hunting skills that the average pet will not.

Do not encourage the chasing of birds and other wildlife when out and about if you want to harness your hunter.

railway lines and then what is around – dogs, people, birds, other animals and so on. This helps me manage my dogs and limits accidental behaviours happening and becoming problematic.

The 'check-in'

I love a 'check-in'. This is when your spaniel looks to you, engages and almost asks 'is this ok?'. They do it very naturally and because so many spaniels seek connection with their handler through eye contact, it is something that we can capture and use to our advantage, especially when it comes to potential hunting behaviour.

Because 'check-ins' are commonly offered, I find it quite easy to 'capture'. Allow them to sniff and explore close to you, stand still for a moment with no forward motion and just see what they do.

Take advantage of training opportunities when out and about to reward calm behaviour in the face of exciting stimuli.

MANAGE YOUR ENVIRONMENT AND USE IT TO YOUR ADVANTAGE

- Get into the habit of checking the ground where you are going to exercise or train your spaniel. This means being aware of rabbits, pheasants or other game birds that might be around.
- For novice dogs in training, walk over the ground first yourself to move game on so that scent is present, but ideally no wildlife. Alternatively, if you have a steady, trained older dog, use it as a training opportunity to run them over the ground first to move any game on before bringing out the youngsters.
- If there is no scent and you are training, pre-bait areas with some food and then work your spaniel onto these areas to work on your managed and connected hunting skills.
- When you are out and opportunities arise – rabbits, hare, pigeons, crows, ducks and so on – providing you have control of your spaniel, use them as opportunities to permit orientation and recognition of their presence, but reward calmness and the ability to re-engage with you, even in the presence of this exciting stimulus. This builds on self-control and their ability to resist temptation.
- After any hunting behaviour, intentional or accidental, take time to calm your spaniel down and allow them to relax, perhaps by putting them back on lead and going for a calm, controlled walk or a couple of controlled and steady retrieves. Hunting is a highly arousing behaviour, so training the 'calm down' afterwards is also important.

The check in is a great way of maintaining connection and engagement with your spaniel.

If they also stop, turn towards you and give you eye contact, mark and reward it, either by throwing a food reward towards them, or even past you. Indeed, animating the reward can make it more exciting and more likely that your spaniel will want to re-engage with you.

I tend not to put auto check-ins on cue. Instead, I capture and reward them when they are offered. Over time, the food reward can be gradually reduced in frequency, but acknowledging the check-in and then giving some form of follow-on cue is helpful. It could be a recall or even permission to carry on what they were doing.

The automatic check-in quickly becomes a way of you and your spaniel remaining connected and engaged with each other when out in exciting environments. It can also effectively help you harness hunting behaviour as a result.

What to do if your spaniel self-hunts

Ideally, with training and management, your spaniel will learn to work with you and under your guidance. They will be practising hunting and scenting, but then also be able to break their behavioural pattern and re-engage with you because that has been heavily rewarded. They will also be at a suitable level of arousal where they are still in full control of their faculties and the 'red mist' has not descended.

However, sometimes it goes wrong. A rabbit pops up when you least expect it. An injured pheasant cannot fly. Or your spaniel has already gone over their functional arousal threshold for another reason and their ability to perform usually robust behaviours is impacted.

Firstly, intervene if you can and get your spaniel under physical control – back on lead. If this is not possible, having an emergency cue is useful. In fact, training an emergency cue and keeping that training 'topped up' regularly is good practice. Your emergency cue should be something that has a history of incredible rewards, and I mean INCREDIBLE. This means that after lots of repetitions, when your dog hears the emergency cue, it cuts through the instinctive hunt mode (or whatever else your dog is doing) and effectively interrupts what they were doing, allowing you both to reconnect and your spaniel to indulge in more suitable behaviours.

However, if self-hunting has become an intense and very practised behaviour, seeking suitable professional training help and support is strongly advised for your own sanity and the safety and welfare of your spaniel and the animals they may come into contact with.

Self-hunting spaniels are a danger to themselves and others around them.

SUCCESS WITHOUT SUPPRESSION

I have heard many spaniel caregivers say, 'if only they didn't sniff', usually accompanied by a pained eye roll. The desire to have a spaniel who is not interested in the scented world around them, or one who on a lovely recall suddenly veers off after a superb sniff is the stuff of dreams for many.

Spaniels are sniffing machines and, while we can attempt to suppress their scenting and hunting, it is rarely successful or indeed fair and ethical to dogs who were bred for this very purpose. Suppression attempts also often employ aversive and punishing methods, which negatively impact not only canine welfare but also the relationship between dog and handler. Suppressed behaviours also have the tendency to pop up when you least expect it. For this reason, I always advocate working with these inherent skills and training the other, essential foundation skills of focus, self-control and the ability to resist temptation.

Hunt ***with*** your spaniel.

If you know there is a scent of rabbits, work with them. Hold your palm flat to the ground saying, 'what's here' and encouraging them to get their nose down. Move around encouraging them to move with you and explore the areas you are highlighting. Scatter some tasty treats that they can then hunt and find or throw a toy into some vegetation that they can then hunt through it under your direction. This allows you to successfully harness hunting behaviour in a controlled and managed way. Your spaniel gets to indulge their natural instincts, and you get successful behavioural management without suppression.

There is nothing better than the spaniel that flushes a rabbit and stops, even momentarily, giving you time to connect with them and respond appropriately – it might be that you recall them back, ask for a stop/sit/wait or get them ready to retrieve said rabbit if you are out working them.

TRAINING AN EMERGENCY RECALL CUE

- This cue should only be used in extreme, emergency situations (calling off a chase, interrupting intense hunting, in a dangerous situation) OR when you are training it.
- In training, every single repetition needs to be rewarded WELL – get out a reward that is amazing and valued by your spaniel – smoked salmon, a sachet of cat food, a toy that they adore, anything that your spaniel will sell their soul for.
- Start on lead or long line in a controlled environment and allow them to amble ahead.
- Saying your emergency cue word (choose something only used for this and even something really odd/unusual – I have 'COOKIES' as mine) and with your incredible reward in your hand, show them and then turn away from your spaniel, luring them with the reward.
- As they turn towards you and engage, throw the reward forwards from you – remember you are both now heading in the opposite direction to where you were originally facing – this rehearses coming away from exciting stimuli.
- Repeat, repeat, repeat and increase the environmental distractions over time.
- Practise this off lead too and also practise it without the reward in your hand, but only giving it after your spaniel has turned towards you and re-engaged.
- Train this skill maybe once or twice a week with three to five repetitions each time, all with the incredible reward to keep the skill 'alive' and the reward value topped up.

This emergency cue uses classical conditioning to develop an almost automatic, non-thinking response in your dog which can be useful for emergency recall or calling off an exciting hunting situation. Instead of a recall, you might train this to be a stop.

Train an emergency cue such as 'stop' or a recall that you can use in extreme situations – use incredible rewards to make it a great choice for your spaniel.

Hunt with your spaniel and make it a joint endeavour, whether it is for working purposes or you are hunting for toys.

TOP TIPS FOR HARNESSING THE HUNTER

- Remember that spaniels were born and bred to hunt.
- Learn to recognise when your spaniel is entering hunting mode through their body language and attitude – this helps you manage them in training and real-life situations.
- Manage your environment, especially when training and before your spaniel's self-control skills are robust – do quick 'risk assessments' of the environment and use leads or long lines.
- Hunting is hugely arousing for our dogs – this can be both a good and a bad thing depending on the context, so manage hunting behaviour carefully – self-hunting often becomes hugely reinforcing for spaniels, so limiting accidental occurrence is critical.
- If you aim to work or compete your spaniel, your hunting needs will differ from the average companion spaniel – you will need to train appropriately and specifically.
- For the companion spaniel, use games and training methods that capture the hunting instinct of our spaniels in a suitable way, such as hunting for food – just be aware that some of these might be conflicting for working or competitive needs.
- Check-ins allow you and your spaniel to keep connected, even in the face of exciting stimuli and distractions – the frequency of auto check-ins also allows you to gauge your spaniel's state of mind – are they thinking or are they starting to become over-aroused by scents and the potential to hunt? Manage appropriately.
- Train and practise an emergency cue that becomes a conditioned response that you can use in a critical and potentially unsafe situation.

MAX

CHAPTER

THE ACTIVE SPANIEL

Spaniels like to do 'stuff.' They tend to be the busy characters of the dog world who thrive on being active and having a 'job' to do. While many spaniels love snoozing and relaxing, they temper this downtime by spending the rest of their time active. Consider activity to be one of the essential 'needs' of a spaniel – fail to meet this need at your peril.

Active spaniels have fun and sometimes win rosettes too.

THE NEED FOR ACTIVITY

Spaniels were originally selectively bred for their working skills as gundogs. They are optimistic and very resilient – essential when working in wet, cold and often difficult environments. Hunting for and retrieving wounded game to your handler through brambles and briars needs a special level of persistence, resilience and bravery.

Unfortunately, this inbuilt persistence and resilience has a downside. Spaniels often do not have a very good 'off' switch and can run themselves to exhaustion – this is of particular concern for spaniels who are unfit and/or exercising in hot conditions. They might not be very good at slowing down or stopping, even when they are fatigued or physically suffering. Springer Spaniels are a breed at particular risk of heat-related illness, probably related to their propensity to remain active, even in extreme conditions. The adrenaline rush that often comes with activity, and especially an enjoyable and rewarding activity can mean that our spaniels push through pain and discomfort, sometimes to their detriment.

Spaniels will frequently exercise to exhaustion – we often need to help them make good decisions.

PUSHING THROUGH PAIN

I remember Molly working in front of me in thick woodland, quartering on the hunt of pheasant to flush. It was a sunny winter day and a lovely one to be out with my dogs. As she whizzed past me, I realised she had a large leaf stuck to her flank and blew my stop whistle so I could remove it.

It was not a leaf. It was a large flap of skin hanging down on her flank with underlying tissues exposed. Was she happy at being stopped? No. Would she have continued to hunt if I had allowed her? Yes. Would that have been a good decision on her part? Absolutely not.

My first cocker, Megan, did something similar one Sunday afternoon when we were out checking estate boundaries and moving pheasant back to where they should be. She ran full pelt into a deer fence, tearing a neat 'L' shape into her chest. Megan also would have continued to work, despite the large wound that was actually interfering with her forward movement.

Both injuries happened out doing what they enjoyed and when their adrenaline was up. Megan was rushed to our local out of hours vet for sedation and stapling. On the way, shock kicked in. By the time we got to the vet (less than an hour) she was a very unhappy spaniel, floppy and whimpering. In Molly's case, my vehicle was parked the best part of a mile away from where we were. I radioed to say I was rushing off to the vet, got the rest of my team on lead and started a speedy walk back to my truck. Initially Molly was trotting along happily, but like Megan, as the adrenaline wore off, she slowed down and started wobbling. I carried her the rest of the way to the truck while on the phone to my vet saying I was on my way after administering initial first aid.

Luckily, both injuries healed well and fast. However, these (and other incidents) highlighted to me the risks our spaniels run, even in a controlled working environment. It has made me hyper-aware of the risks they run in a less controlled situation (think free running or self-hunting in a woodland) and if they were to be injured when I was less able to respond in a timely manner.

Sometimes we do need to save our spaniels from themselves and be aware that they might not always be able to advocate for themselves or recognise when their own health and wellbeing is at stake.

Hunting and retrieving

Hunting and retrieving are fundamental spaniel activities. This means that when left to their own devices, many spaniels will go 'self-employed', actively hunting, often for the local wildlife.

Many spaniel caregivers will report the need for their spaniel to carry an item almost all the time. The need to carry something in their mouth is often pronounced during an exciting situation such as visitors arriving or getting ready to go for a walk. Many spaniels will opt to carry something when they are worried or otherwise conflicted about a situation.

It is also the case that many spaniels simply spend much of their awake time carrying something (shoes and slippers especially) – it is instinctive and self-rewarding. Even the smaller and toy spaniel breeds such as the Cavalier King Charles Spaniel will retain hunting and retrieving skills.

This all means that we must remember that spaniels have physical and psychological energy to burn. Restricting activity can result in a very unhappy spaniel – one that is physically unfit (detrimental to their overall health, wellbeing and longevity), bored, frustrated and even distressed. This often results in destructive behaviour – either of their surroundings or sadly, sometimes of themselves. Other behavioural

Carrying things, especially shoes, is a typical spaniel behaviour.

challenges such as problematic separation-related behaviours or stereotypies (repetitive behaviours such as pacing, often seen in captive animals in zoos) may arise if our spaniels do not have a suitable outlet for their energy and enthusiasm.

For any spaniel caregiver, remembering what spaniels were originally bred for is essential to meet their needs and ensure your relationship is as enjoyable and mutually beneficial as possible. While you might not have any desire to work your spaniel as a gundog, providing them with a suitable outlet for their natural, inbuilt skills and abilities goes a long way to meeting their physical and psychological needs.

Luckily, there are a number of activities and sporting disciplines that you can explore with your spaniel, from traditional gundog work and training, to some of the newer canine activities such as hoopers or canine freestyle. They will be happy training and taking part in whatever you choose, but giving your spaniel a 'job' is a great way to keep them (and by definition, you) very happy and fulfilled indeed.

GIVE YOUR SPANIEL A JOB!

Finding a suitable outlet for your active spaniel should not be too difficult. You might be inclined to walk them for miles and miles each day in an effort to tire them out, but lots of physical exercise will simply make an already naturally active dog physically fitter. Striking a balance between exercising their body and brain will go a long way to living harmoniously with a happy, fulfilled spaniel. You might even like the idea of challenging yourselves against other dogs in competition, ranging from local, fun dog shows and events to international competitions in your chosen discipline(s).

You do not need to compete in order to gain the benefits of activity. You can start at home and capture some of their natural skills to incorporate into your day-to-day life, although specialist and experienced training for many activities is strongly recommended. This will ensure you are both learning 'best practice' and the safest way to take part in your chosen activities. It also means that should you wish to progress

Giving your spaniel a job can help keep them physically and psychologically healthy.

Being able to settle around distractions and exciting situations is essential.

towards competitive standards, you will have a good foundation in the essential skills and expectations.

If your aim is simply to have a pleasurable, enjoyable and well-behaved companion with whom you have a great partnership, training fundamental life skills will be key. These skills also form the foundation for any other specific training you might aspire to do with your spaniel and should be regularly revisited and reinforced throughout life too.

REWARD, REWARD, REWARD

Whatever activity you choose to undertake with your spaniel, reward them to reinforce the desired behaviours. In most canine disciplines, modern training methods are underpinned by positive reinforcement methods, using food or toys to reinforce and reward specific behaviours.

Food is often the easiest way to reward clarity and precision, which is important for 'clean' skills in many activities. Verbal and physical praise can also be used, but note that in some cases and for some individual dogs, physical touch can be detrimental and disliked, especially during activities that are high arousal.

My own spaniels are all incredibly food oriented and work really well for food rewards. I use food as a reward system when training new specific skills and behaviours, especially ones where I am close to my dog. However, when working as gundogs, being allowed to hunt or retrieve is actually a better reward than food, so they will become my chosen rewards in that situation. With a little bit of consideration and watching your own dog, you will be able to work out a hierarchy of rewards for specific skills, behaviours, contexts and situations. This helps you tailor your training specifically.

For many activities and for working and competing dogs, your spaniel will need to be able to work for prolonged periods of time without reward. It is important to build duration to any behaviour and create internal motivation in your dog to continue to perform specific skills. In most competitive environments, food and toy rewards are not permitted and can only be given after the completion of competition work. This means that teaching and developing delayed gratification in your spaniel is important – good things come to those who demonstrate the skills asked for!

Good things come to those who wait.

GETTING ACTIVE AT HOME

Home is the best place to start introducing activities, whether they are a tiny puppy, a mature adult or even a distinguished senior. Capture default behaviours that your spaniel does at home, and this makes training part of your daily routine, rather than something that you need to allocate hours each week to.

At home, encourage and reward a great retrieve pattern by encouraging your spaniel to carry items and deliver them to your hands. This might be shoes, socks, or anything else that might find its way into a spaniel's mouth! Rewarding well for giving you things will stand you in good stead, should your spaniel even get hold of something they should not have. If their reinforcement history for giving things up to you has been consistently good, then the likelihood of them 'acquiring' and potentially becoming possessive over items is significantly reduced. By encouraging your spaniel to give you items directly into your hand, you minimise the chance of them deciding not to give the item up, dropping it and going on their way, or picking up something else. You are also instilling good habits that will prove critical if you decide to work or compete your spaniel where delivery to hand is expected.

My own spaniels regularly 'help' load and unload the washing machine. It does take at least twice as long as it otherwise would, but as a training exercise incorporated into daily chores, it is hugely valuable, and they enjoy it. I also ask them to 'find my slippers/shoes' – an almost constantly repeated refrain.

Capture their natural hunting and scenting behaviour at home by scatter-feeding either on the floor or in the garden. This can keep a spaniel occupied for several minutes and is great as a gentle form of physical exercise, but still using their brain. This is an ideal activity for young puppies who might be restricted in how much physical exercise they can do, or for our older, perhaps slightly less mobile spaniels.

An empty cardboard box with scrunched up paper inside and food treats scattered inside is a simple and inexpensive enrichment hunting/sniffing activity. Alternatively, a ball pit or other bespoke toys such as snuffle mats are available to create controlled but interesting and enjoyable hunting and sniffing challenges.

When out walking, scatter some treats into long grass (be selective where you do this for safety and to avoid litter, faecal matter, or other potential contamination) or hide toys and encourage your spaniel to find them. Hiding favourite toys around the house or garden can be a fun task for you to set for your spaniel. This adds stimulation and activity when time

Reward your spaniel for bringing you things they 'find'!

Household tasks can make for interesting training opportunities.

Scatter feeding is an easy way to encourage gentle activity and allow them to sniff, which is inherently relaxing.

Cockers waiting to pick up on a working shoot day.

might be limited, or you are restricted in being able to get outdoors because of poor weather or darkness during the winter months.

Giving your spaniel a job of some sort and especially one that you can 'do' together is a great way of working with them in a positive way and giving them a constructive outlet for some of their most inherent behaviours.

GUNDOG WORK AND TRAINING

Working gundogs remain a key fixture of the countryside and are an essential part of the shooting field, responsible for hunting, finding and flushing 'game' (typically game birds such as pheasant and partridge, but might also include rabbits and waterfowl such as ducks). This job of hunting and flushing is called 'beating,' as the handlers will walk through the undergrowth with their dogs, 'beating' the cover with sticks and making noises to encourage the movement of game. The next essential role is retrieving shot and wounded game as quickly and cleanly as possible to their handler – 'picking up.' Gundogs are essential colleagues on the shooting field.

It is clear that the traditional work of gundogs can attract discussion and debate. Many spaniel caregivers are uncomfortable with the idea of handling shot game and have no desire to work their dog in this capacity. However, it is useful to be aware of the expectations of the working spaniel and while your own spaniel might never see, smell or hear gunshot, the ancestry is there and does form a robust foundation for many instinctive behaviours. Appreciating this and what it would mean for a working gundog can be hugely helpful in understanding the spaniel you live with.

Equally, you might have ambitions to learn more about the job that your spaniel was bred to do and aspire to one day work them in the field. Many first-time spaniel caregivers do get bitten by the gundog bug, and before long have a 4×4 vehicle, more than one spaniel and a wardrobe full of wellies and muted greens and browns.

The working spaniel

The typical gundog breeds and types tend to have particular specialities to make them suitable for specific roles and environments encountered on the shooting field. Spaniels were the hunters with a capacity to hunt through dense plant material, using their finely honed noses to locate game species by scent. Once found, the game is 'flushed' to the 'gun' (the person with the shotgun). A well-trained spaniel will stop to the flush and not chase. If the shot is successful, there might then be an opportunity for the spaniel to find and retrieve the shot bird or animal.

Spaniels are often valued as being 'all-rounders,' capable of turning their 'paw' to a number of essential tasks on the shooting field, but they will often be found working happily alongside other gundog breeds and types (and even some non-traditional breeds such as terriers or collies) too. Even out of the traditional shooting season for game (which only takes place within specific calendar periods) many gundogs fulfil working roles in the preparation for the shooting season.

Attributes of the working spaniel

There are some essential attributes of the working spaniel. They should be 'steady,' meaning they do not chase game or run off to make a retrieve unless asked to. When we talk about 'steadiness' in spaniels, this is what we are referring to. A spaniel that is 'gun shy' (where the sound and sometimes scent of gunshot can cause anxiety and fear in extreme cases) will certainly not enjoy the shooting field and be unlikely to work satisfactorily. Being 'gun shy' can have a genetic basis but can also be a result of negative early experiences, so do introduce the sound of shot carefully, especially to young spaniels.

Working dogs also need to be fit, both physically and cognitively to be able to respond to whistle and voice cues, often in poor weather, at a distance and in the face of a host of other exciting distractions. It is also expected that working gundogs are 'mute' and do not make noise – certainly not any excess noise. This includes whining, yipping and barking. For some spaniels, this is really difficult and can be a trait of certain breeding lines or the result of frustration and excitement.

The working spaniel needs to have a 'good nose' and the desire to hunt for game, both to flush and then also to retrieve. This hunting will usually take place in dense undercover and in sometimes very harsh and unforgiving conditions, meaning the working spaniel needs to be relatively insensitive to physical discomfort and have the tenacity to work in less than pleasant situations. A willingness to hunt and then retrieve fur and feather – sometimes off water – is also important for the working spaniel, although sometimes the retrieving is left to the retrieving breeds and the spaniels' role is simply the hunting and flushing. I know of several spaniels who prefer to hunt than retrieve and they fulfil this role well.

The working gundog needs to be steady.

Several of my own spaniels appear to deeply enjoy the hunting and retrieving aspect of their work and I need to manage them carefully to ensure they are doing what they need to do and what they have been asked to do. It is poor etiquette for a dog to take a retrieve from someone else or to hunt beyond the area they have been asked to cover, but this is sometimes a challenge for an enthusiastic spaniel, and their handler may have to offer sincere and profuse apologies!

Most importantly, the working gundog needs to be highly adaptable and comfortable in a range of situations, places and around unfamiliar dogs and people. On many shoot days, the working dogs will travel together in close proximity, often in unfamiliar vehicles – rarely will any of them grumble.

One key aspect about working your spaniel is that it can be an amazing way to build your relationship. A huge amount of trust (not to mention the hours spent together training) is needed between you both. You will also meet like-minded people in the countryside and get the opportunity to visit many wonderful places that are not typically for public access. You might even get to cook and eat the spoils of your day out working your spaniel, should you desire.

Gundog tests, trials and scurries

There are competitive opportunities related to gundog work that take place almost all year round. Field trials are the competitive pinnacle of the gundog world and run in the same format as a working shoot day, with competing dogs and handlers demonstrating the skills and attributes expected when working. Live game and shot will be involved, and the standards and expectations are high. In the UK, there are different competitive levels and competitive classes, based on the standard of handler and dog, as well as the breed of spaniel.

Gundog working tests are similar to trials but take place during the spring and summer months and involve canvas dummies for retrieving and starter pistols firing 'blanks' instead of real gunshot. Working tests can be a useful way to test your training in a competitive arena without the pressure of a trial environment or live game – although be aware, they do tend to take place in areas where game might be found! I recall a good friend working her spaniel in a test and she was struggling to keep him in an area for hunting in front of the judges. This turned out to be because he had scented a pheasant and preferred to hunt for that instead of the comparatively boring canvas dummy he was supposed to be finding.

Gundog working tests are competitive events in which you can test your spaniel's hunting and retrieving skills without the pressure of live game.

Gundog scurries are the speedy, fun versions of gundog work and are often found at countryside events. They take the form of different challenges involving retrieving and have a timed component. Your dog might be asked to retrieve dummies or tennis balls from an alley containing straw bales as obstacles to be jumped on the way out to retrieve and on the way back with the retrieve. If you have a fast, reliable spaniel who loves to retrieve, scurries are a thoroughly enjoyable way to show off their skills. There are often good prizes on offer for successful scurry dogs and handlers too.

Gundog training

Even if you have no desire to work your spaniel or be involved in field sports, you might still be interested in aspects of the training, especially if you might like to take part in gundog working tests and scurries. It is also useful, certainly for spaniels bred from working lines, to appreciate their inherent skills and how to work with these rather than against them. Gundog-style training can help channel those skills in a positive way.

Much gundog training is done using canvas dummies for retrieving. This means that if you would rather not have contact with other birds or animals, then dummy work is an option. You can easily reach a high level of competence by training on dummies alone and there are competitive opportunities on dummies only also.

Finding an experienced coach/trainer/instructor who knows and understands your breed will help. Many trainers specialise in specific breeds. It is also good to find someone who supports your aims and ambitions and is aligned with your training ideas and philosophies too – this can go a long way to ensure that you and your dog are happy and confident within a training situation. If your aims are a happy, confident companion, then a trainer experienced in aspects of gundog work but with an appreciation of the needs of a companion dog will be ideal. If you aspire to work your spaniel in the shooting field, or aim to compete in tests and field trials, a trainer experienced in those areas is a good choice.

Gundog work, training and competing tends to be traditional and there is etiquette worth knowing. Some of the terms are also unique to the gundog world, so a trainer who can help you decipher terms such as 'blinds', 'marks' and 'blinking retrieves' is important.

OBEDIENCE AND RALLY

'Obedience' and 'Rally' are two activities that can build on training basics and start your exploration into the competition ring. Sometimes the term 'obedience' is disliked, especially when we consider working with our dog as a partnership, rather than one in which our dogs should be 'obedient' to us, but the elements of obedience as a discipline underpin life skills for our spaniels, as well as forming the basis of all other canine activities.

Both obedience and rally are suitable for spaniels and handlers of all ages, shapes and sizes. Competitively, there are different levels of achievement, making it possible to progress based on your ability. Some training classes will also offer non-competitive achievement awards for 'Canine Good Citizens and Companions', which offer the opportunity to develop your skills to specific levels in your standard class environment.

Obedience

Obedience is all about handler and dog working in harmony through a range of different skills from heelwork to send-aways. Heelwork when done well with the dog maintaining a close and consistent position irrespective of their handler's speed and movement, is a delight to watch. Providing you have consistent performance in the exercises required, absolute precision in obedience is not needed for success at the lower levels. The important part of obedience is the communication between dog and handler and performing set exercises quietly, cleanly and with little fuss. With progression through competitive levels, the number of cues (verbal and visual) permitted is reduced and treats and toys cannot be carried or given in the ring, so proofing your spaniel's skills of behaviour duration with minimal cues and delayed reward is essential.

If you wish to progress competitively, or for your own personal challenge, then developing skills in heelwork, retrieving, send-away (where you send them to a specific location), distance control (where they are asked to perform behaviours such as sit, down and stand at a distance from you) and scent discrimination are all integral to obedience.

Rally

Rally is a canine activity that evolved from obedience. In rally, dog and handler negotiate a set course of signposted 'stations' that direct the handler what the exercise is that they must perform. These exercises can be static (sit, down, stand, for example) or moving (changing direction or pace, for example). As with obedience, there are different levels of achievement and difficulty, making it a good option for developing skills in spaniels of all ages.

AGILITY

Agility is one of the most popular and fastest-growing canine activities. Spaniels are increasingly common participants in the lower height categories. Agility attracts lots of attention and is a common crowd pleaser at shows and outdoor events.

Rally involves following a course of defined instructions.

Agility began in the 1970s as a demonstration event and was modelled on equine events. The essential components of jumps, tunnels, weaves and contact equipment are still seen today, but agility has evolved significantly and now thousandths of a second will make the difference between first and tenth places in competitive classes.

Agility essentials

Agility involves dog and handler negotiating a set course of equipment in the fastest time possible with no faults or elimination. Dogs need to be responsive to their handler and undertake athletic movements quickly and safely. Agility requires training, control and a partnership between dog and person to ensure the correct course is taken.

Jumping competitive classes only involve jumps, tunnels and weaves with no contact equipment. Agility classes include contact equipment of A-frame, seesaw and dog-walk, all of which need careful training so that your dog negotiates them safely and contacts the required 'contact' areas. Failure to contact the required zones on equipment will be faulted by the judge, as will missing any piece of equipment, or traversing it incorrectly.

Spaniels often do well in agility because they can be athletic and speedy. Agility separates dogs based on height classification (by measuring the height of the dog to their withers) and this determines the height of jumps to be negotiated. Different spaniel breeds will range from small to large height categories, although most will fall into medium height and, depending on skill and experience, there are different competitive progression categories too.

Agility training

Like many disciplines, it is a good idea to identify a specialist trainer or classes. This means you will learn on current equipment, suitable surfaces and under current competitive expectations and regulations. This goes a long way to keeping your dog safe. Your dog should be confident off lead, too – training agility on lead is unsafe and not good practice. Your spaniel should be physically mature and able to undertake the high intensity and high impact activities involved.

Agility involves correctly negotiating a course of equipment in the fastest time without faults or elimination.

Dogs need to be physically capable of the demands of activity.

Limiting jumping until a dog is a year old is good practice and for competitive agility, dogs need to be at least eighteen months old, although much foundation work can be done with younger dogs.

DANCING WITH YOUR DOG: HEELWORK TO MUSIC, CANINE FREESTYLE AND TRICK TRAINING

If being a little more creative with your dog training appeals to you, or dance and dramatics are other interests, then combining performance with training and tricks might be an ideal activity. Trick training is a great way to work that eager spaniel brain, as well as get some nifty moves to impress friends and family – you might even end up as stars on screen! Incorporating obedience moves and tricks to music, and if you are so

Tricks can be static poses as well as more active moves.

inclined, throwing some shapes yourself at the same time as cueing your dog to perform behaviours can rapidly get you into the realms of 'dancing' with your dog.

Trick training

Much trick training is simply building on existing skills that your dog will have. Giving a paw can be functional (for drying or nail clipping, for example) but when paired with music or other moves, that simple behaviour can take on a whole new meaning. Trick training is a good way to challenge your spaniel's brain and body, but without the intensity or impact of agility, for example. This means that trick training is ideal for younger and older spaniels, or those recovering from injury. Contrary to popular belief, you can teach older dogs new tricks too, and many older dogs thoroughly enjoy working with their person to learn new things, coupled with fun rewards.

Trick training can be as simple or as complex as you wish, and your spaniel is capable of. Simple tricks include giving a paw, a high five, doing a twist or a spin and weaving through your legs. If you start to combine these, you can quickly create a chain of tricks and a full routine to demonstrate your shared skills.

Dancing with your spaniel

Heelwork to music and canine freestyle are activities performed to a suitable piece of music. Dog and handler need to work as a partnership and showcase their abilities, while including suitable and accurate content of movements and tricks and demonstrating musical interpretation.

Freestyle is 'freer' in its expectations and includes more trick-like movements, including those performed at a distance from the handler. Heelwork to music requires specific heelwork positions to be performed for the majority of the routine, with a few moves incorporated to permit transitions between positions.

Heelwork to music and freestyle training and competition attracts a huge diversity of dog breeds and types because the routines are devised by the handler and can be made to suit individual abilities and skills. This makes them inclusive activities and many spaniels enjoy the opportunity to work closely with their person performing a range of behaviours in quick succession, usually with toy or food rewards at the end (and outside the competition ring).

Find a specialist trainer who understands the discipline well and the regulations that apply, especially if you would like to compete. This is because there are specific movements considered to be unsafe, as well as other aspects such as choosing (and editing) suitable music for your routine. Your spaniel's welfare is a key priority. A good trainer will recognise what their capabilities are and help you design routines to maximise and highlight those.

WORKING TRIALS

Working trials originated from the work that military and law enforcement dogs were expected to undertake including athleticism, nosework, obedience and teamwork. It is an outdoor activity, so ideal for handlers and spaniels who relish an opportunity to test their skills in the open air, and comprises nosework, agility and control sections of competitive tests. These will include heelwork, tracking and nosework to find hidden items and agility over set obstacles.

Outdoor activities are ideal for spaniels.

There are different expectations at the different competitive levels of working trials, but the basic exercises include:

- Nosework following a pre-laid trail with items to be recovered. There is also a search square exercise where items are found and retrieved.
- Control exercises include heelwork, stays in sit and down, retrieving, barking on cue and steadiness to gunshot at some levels.
- Agility which involves three obstacles – a hurdle jump, an upright wooden scale, and a long jump.

If your spaniel has good basic obedience skills and also has some nosework and agility skills, then working trials could be a fun and challenging way to combine them. Your spaniel needs to be happy to work around other dogs, as much of the work is undertaken off lead.

Specialist support and training for working trials is advised. It tends to be quite a niche activity too, so getting involved in the training and competitive community is highly recommended so that you can get a real insight into working trials.

SCENT WORK AND MANTRAILING

We know that the olfactory capability of dogs is easily several thousand times better than our own. The dog's nose is able to detect chemical compounds at vanishingly low concentrations and with a high degree of accuracy. Highly trained detection dogs can recognise and discriminate between different odours at almost 100 per cent accuracy and are sometimes better than specialised laboratory detection machinery.

We are still learning about the amazing power of the dog's nose and exploring ways to employ it, but we can also use scenting as a form of active enrichment. A number of fun and functional activities are available to take part in, where your dog's scenting skills can be honed and challenged. For spaniels who naturally like to hunt and the ability to locate game using their noses is a key skill, sniffing as an activity makes sense.

Sniffing is also an enjoyable, enriching and even relaxing activity for dogs. It can be useful to help dogs learn to focus and because it is a skill that all dogs have, it is an activity that suits spaniels of all ages and abilities. This means that doing basic scentwork at home is achievable, looking for food or a favourite toy using their nose. Snuffle mats and scatter feeding are great ways to encourage your dog to use their nose to find food. Scatter feeding is a useful enrichment activity and is easily done by throwing some dry food, grated cheese, or similar, onto a clean surface.

Scentwork training

There are many training classes offering scentwork as a specialist activity. Basic scentwork training often starts by encouraging your dog to find a piece of food or a favoured toy before progressing to specific odours. You can then develop your skill sets in searching different locations and your dog's indication style, which needs to be clear and consistent, especially for working or competitive ambitions.

A passive indication is where your dog 'freezes' in a set position, which could be a sit, down or stand, without touching the source of the scent. This is typically encouraged for working scent-detection dogs when the source of the scent might be harmful, dangerous or something that could be contaminated if touched. On the other hand, an active indication will often involve your dog indicating the location of scent by barking, nosing at, pawing at or even retrieving a scented item. If you have aims to compete, check what the expectations will be for competing in terms of indication and the same applies for any working detection aspirations too.

Sniffing is a great activity for our spaniels, whether for work or for fun.

Mantrailing

Mantrailing builds on our dogs' scenting ability and involves locating a 'misper' (missing person) by tracking a scent trail. If you fancy having a go at mantrailing, finding an experienced instructor is a good idea to get clear guidance and support. It is an activity that encompasses a good amount of walking, especially as you both become more proficient and track longer and older scent trails. Mantrailing is a great activity to take part in with your spaniel, as it builds and enhances your relationship and is dependent on you having trust and confidence in each other.

One benefit of scentwork and mantrailing is that they tend to be individual activities in which dog and handler are working independently of other dogs and not in close proximity. This can make the different forms of scentwork ideal for spaniels that are worried by, or not very social with other dogs (or even people).

CANICROSS, BIKEJOR AND SLED DOG SPORTS

While spaniels are obviously not traditional sled dogs, if they take part in activities such as canicross and bikejor, they are classed as sled dogs! These activities developed for the need to keep sled dogs fit and active out of the snowy season, and their handlers ('mushers') developed ways to do this by running, skiing and biking with their dogs. The important distinction is that in these activities, the dog is attached to their handler, or the bike, and is providing some additional pulling power.

Running with your spaniel

It is possible to run with your spaniel off lead, running beside you on lead or attached to you with a specialist harness for them and belt for you. Obviously, any free running spaniel should be responsive to you and stay close in the face of distractions and in suitable environments.

Running on lead can work well too if your pace and your spaniel's pace are similar. Being pulled by your spaniel when you are holding a lead is not pleasant for you or them, whether the lead is attached to their collar or a harness. Holding a lead can also interfere with your running style.

My own team and I run regularly, covering distances up to 15km (9 miles) at a steady pace. I am not a natural or fast runner, but I thoroughly enjoy plodding along with my spaniel teammates. Usually this is a mix of free running in safe places and canicross when more control is needed, so they are attached to me by bungee lines to their harnesses but pull out in front of me. Running with my spaniels is definitely a good way of exercising us both and meeting their needs for movement, activity and sometimes simply running in a controlled and managed way. If you fancy taking part in races, you can do this too, whether specialist canicross races, or dog-friendly regular running races. We have taken part in some beautiful runs in amazing places. We even have some blingy medals to prove it!

Canicross and canihiking

Canicross is where dog and person run together as a connected team. The dog pulls out in front of their person, mimicking sled dogs pulling sleds. Canihiking is the same, although done at a more sedate pace, often over more uneven terrain.

If your spaniel is physically fit and able, running can be a wonderful outlet for them and a great way to strengthen your relationship through shared experiences. Because canicross means your spaniel is connected to you, it can be useful in areas where dogs must be under close control or on lead but is also useful if your recall is not consistent.

Canicross races often come with medals.

Be aware that not every dog enjoys running or moving at speed, and if your dog is lagging behind, stopping, or otherwise showing behaviours indicating they are not enjoying themselves, they could be tired, injured or just no longer having fun. Work as a team and look out for each other. Perhaps your spaniel prefers to sniff and take their time when exercising, or they are older, less fit or recovering from illness or injury. In these cases, they are unlikely to enjoy prolonged activity, but cani-hiking might be an option. Canisports can be intense for our spaniels and dogs should be physically mature before starting. Usual guidance is that you should not do any serious canisport activity until your dog is twelve to eighteen months old and, for older dogs, or those with health concerns, consider your chosen activity carefully. Always start slowly and build up distances and speed gently.

Bikejoring

Bikejoring is where your spaniel is connected to your bike and pulls out in front. It is usually undertaken on forestry tracks and other suitable locations. You usually need permission and permits to bikejor, and it is not suitable for public areas. Suitable insurance is also strongly recommended because bikejoring is great fun but potentially dangerous too – always wear a cycle helmet and other protection in case of falls. If bikejoring is something you fancy, definitely get some specialised help, advice and training and an extra set of hands is always helpful to get you and your dog going.

Canisport equipment

For canisports, getting the correct kit is strongly recommended and receiving specialist help for fitting is a good idea to keep you and your spaniel safe and comfortable. A good pair of running shoes is essential and trail shoes will provide addition traction and grip – essential if you have a strong-pulling spaniel.

Your dog will need a suitable harness – a different one to their usual walking one if used is a good idea so they can differentiate what activity they are doing. You will need a specialised belt that sits around your hips and buttocks – this is connected to your spaniel via an elasticated bungee line. The equipment is intended to make running with your spaniel as safe, easy and effective as possible.

OTHER ACTIVITIES AND DISCIPLINES

There are many more activities that you can explore with your spaniel too, some with specialist training and competitive opportunities. There are others that are in development and gradually gaining in popularity and increased participation. Here are other activities to consider.

Canicross is a team activity and a great way to exercise you and your spaniel(s).

Specialist kit is needed for canicross to ensure comfort for you and your spaniel.

Hoopers is an increasingly popular activity.

Flyball

Flyball is a team relay race in which dogs race each other over a short series of jumps to collect a ball and return to their handler. The fastest team with no faults wins. It is a fast and furious canine activity and can be really noisy, too. Participating dogs get incredibly excited and tend to let the world know about it. For spaniels who love running and balls, flyball is a perfect option and the height and speed of many spaniels can make them valuable additions in a team.

Hoopers

Hoopers is similar to agility where dog and handler negotiate a course of obstacles such as tunnels, barrels and hoops rather than jumps. Speed and accuracy are important, as well as getting around a course with no faults. Hoopers is often a good choice for spaniels who cannot jump for health reasons, or are retired from agility, although it is very much a discipline in its own right, too.

TOP TIPS FOR YOUR ACTIVE SPANIEL

- Be critical about your spaniel's health and physical fitness before undertaking a new activity and introduce it gradually, building up intensity of training over a period of time.
- Young puppies can start foundation training for many canine activities, but take care not to do too much long-duration, intense or high-impact exercise or activity before they are physically mature.
- If you or your spaniel are recovering from illness or injury, do chat to your doctor or vet before starting any new activity, especially those that are physically demanding.
- It is worth spending time and money on specialised support, training and equipment for many canine activities – this will ensure you are following current and best practice and will probably save you money in the long term.
- While it is great to be active, do make sure you factor in rest periods and more relaxed activities for your spaniel too, and training them to be able to settle and relax is also an important life skill.
- Have fun! Whatever you do choose to do, it should be enjoyable for you both.

CHAPTER 10

SURVIVING SPANIELS

It is perhaps inaccurate to title this chapter 'Surviving Spaniels', because they bring so much joy, companionship, fun, activity, laughter and opportunity into our lives. Having a spaniel join you and your family should be so much more than simply something to be survived.

Having said that, there are potential challenges that come with sharing your life with a spaniel. These can feel overwhelming and confusing, especially for the novice. Hopefully, this book has given you some hints, tips and advice to create an enriching and pleasurable lifetime with your spaniel, whether you are in the first few days of 'spanieldom' or a veteran with the breed.

Here, we explore some common questions and queries that spaniel caregivers raise. Some are spaniel-specific, while others apply equally to all dogs.

First, let's examine some key principles to help you 'survive your spaniel'.

Spaniels make for loyal, fun and devoted family members.

BE CALM AND CLEAR

The ability to be calm (or to fake calmness!) is a useful skill around spaniels. These big canine personalities in medium-sized bodies, can veer dramatically between comatose and whirlwind. These extreme fluctuations can be unsettling, but with a clear and calm approach to managing your spaniel and helping them learn what is and what is not acceptable, you can foster a solid relationship.

Many spaniels react to situations, rather than a more measured and thoughtful response. This is what we have selectively bred spaniels to do – act first, think later. We can teach our spaniels to be mindful in how they respond to particular stimuli, whether that is a moving object or something else of interest. Part of that training is also in how we respond and react to the world around us. Some of the best handlers I have seen (and try to emulate) barely say a word and rarely raise their voice.

There is a serenity about their handling which is deliberate with little ambiguity. This helps your spaniel develop a more thoughtful response to the multitude

Build trust and connection with your spaniel for a great partnership.

of stimuli around them and will help you work more effectively as a team, whether your spaniel is a family member, a sporting teammate, or a working colleague. Spaniels often mirror your behaviour – indeed this is a behavioural attribute well studied in a range of species. The behaviour of those around us reflects how we behave. Equally, training our dogs is about so much more than simply getting a desired behaviour. It is about building trust and connection, allowing your spaniel to be able to say, 'I'm not sure' or 'I'm a bit worried about that' and them knowing that you will respect that and help them.

Be calm and clear with your spaniel and in whatever you ask them to do. It goes a long way in ensuring you have a companion with an outlook and approach similar to your own.

BE FIRM BUT FAIR

Clarity in our expectations makes it easier for our spaniels to know if what they are doing is right or not. Firm boundaries are critical. It is not about being harsh. It is making it explicitly clear what the expectation is, demonstrating how your spaniel can meet it and rewarding them appropriately, while also creating an environment in which they thrive.

You might decide that you do not want your spaniel upstairs. Initially, you need to manage the environment so that your spaniel cannot accidentally get access upstairs – easily done with a stairgate. The clarity of boundary is firm but fair and you can reward your spaniel for remaining at the correct side of the boundary. Over time, the habit is built that the stairs are just not somewhere for your spaniel to go. This can become so robust that you might be able to dispense with the stairgate.

If you do not manage the environment or have other household members who let your spaniel head upstairs occasionally, do not be surprised if that behaviour becomes repeated. It is not then fair to reprimand your spaniel when there are no clear and firm boundaries or expectations.

Being firm and fair is as much about being respectful, empathetic and compassionate in your interactions with your spaniel. It can also help to accelerate learning and create robust behavioural habits.

Clear boundaries and expectations in your interactions make it easier for your spaniel to know what is and what is not acceptable.

KINDNESS IS KEY

It might sound trite, but being kind is underappreciated in our interactions with dogs. Taking a kind approach in everything we do with our spaniels means we can appreciate them as individuals and as fellow sentient beings who are aware of the world around them in the same way as we are. Dogs have limited agency to make decisions for themselves – we regulate and manage so much of their daily lives. Simple things such as allowing choice to participate in activities or management techniques through cooperative care and showing you are aware of them and how they feel, are cornerstones to a kind approach.

Kindness and understanding helps us bond. Because spaniels thrive on human contact and connection, kindness is the least we can do in a world that is distinctly human-centric and one in which our spaniels need to undertake significant adaptions in order to cope.

COMMON QUESTIONS AND QUERIES FROM SPANIEL CAREGIVERS

Whether you are new to spaniels or a seasoned spaniel handler, there some common queries, relating to feeding, management and training spaniels.

Spaniels are sentient beings and deserve to be treated fairly and kindly.

How do I stop my spaniel...... [insert behaviour here]

When we live with dogs, or any other living being, sometimes they do things that annoy us. It is sobering then to think that we will also do things that annoy them – that is the nature of relationships. When we bring a dog into our home, we forget they do not speak our language. They are a different species with specific needs and that we need to help them understand our world, our expectations and our language too.

One of the biggest challenges that many caregivers face is stopping their spaniel indulging in behaviours that are unwanted. You just need to pop onto social media and explore any dog training group to see the questions appear – how do I stop my puppy biting? How do I stop my dog jumping on me? How do I stop my dog pulling on the lead? For spaniel caregivers, common queries include – how do I stop my spaniel picking up things? How do I stop my spaniel hunting? How do I stop my spaniel jumping up?

These are always difficult questions for trainers to address. The answer is 'it depends.' It depends on factors such as your spaniel's previous training and experience.

How do I stop my spaniel from…?

Has the behaviour been reinforced and rewarded before (intentionally or accidentally)? Are your spaniel's needs being met? Does your spaniel have a health issue making the undesirable behaviour more likely and the desired behaviour more difficult? What is your spaniel's emotional state when the behaviour occurs?

The other significant point about questions about stopping specific behaviours such as jumping, pulling, free hunting and not recalling, is that often the caregiver wants (whether they really are aware of it or not) a quick fix, that is something that they can do there and then to stop the behaviour. When a trainer starts to assess what is going on and identifies that to develop a new, incompatible and alternative behaviour will take time, work, repetition and management to prevent rehearsing of the undesirable behaviour, many caregivers get frustrated. This can result in further behavioural deterioration, relationship breakdown between spaniel and their person(s) and in extreme cases, rehoming.

So, if you have one (or more) of those behaviours presenting in your spaniel that you would like to stop, what can you do?

Reframe the question

A useful strategy is to reframe the question. Instead of what you DON'T want your spaniel to do, what behaviour WOULD you like? It is usually the direct opposite to the behaviour you dislike.

For example, if your spaniel is jumping on you and you want the jumping to stop, the opposite and preferred behaviour is keeping all four feet on the floor. Once you have identified the preferred behaviour, you can then manage the situation to get that behaviour, then reward and reinforce it. In the case of jumping, be 'armed' with a handful of treats or a toy and as they go to jump on you, drop the treats or toy on the floor. Timing is critical, and ideally the reward comes before they jump on you.

Once you have the behaviour you do want, repeat, repeat, repeat and reward, reward, reward. Eventually your spaniel realises that keeping four on the floor means nice things appear there and that jumping gets nothing.

These puppies are learning to be calm and settled.

Analyse why the behaviour is happening

When you are faced with a behaviour that you do not like, think carefully about why it is happening. All behaviour has a purpose, even if it might not be obvious to us. The spaniel that barks in response to a neighbourhood dog has learned that barking at that dog makes them go away – that is a good thing because, for some reason, that dog is disliked. I have had this with a local dog who would repetitively approach my dogs when they were in my vehicle. This was quite threatening behaviour for my dogs, who started to negatively respond to the presence of this dog. Frustratingly, it kept occurring and my dogs started to react to the sound of that dog's tag jingling if he came near us. Management ended up being the only strategy. I could not alter the behaviour of the dog or their person, so instead I amended how my dogs were entering and leaving my vehicle, as well as scanning my driveway before doing so for the presence of that dog, rewarding all relaxed behaviours shown by my own dogs.

Sometimes behaviours appear because our spaniel's needs are not being met – activity, movement, hunting, retrieving and so on. The spaniel that self-hunts? They are meeting their internal drives and needs. The spaniel who starts to become possessive over

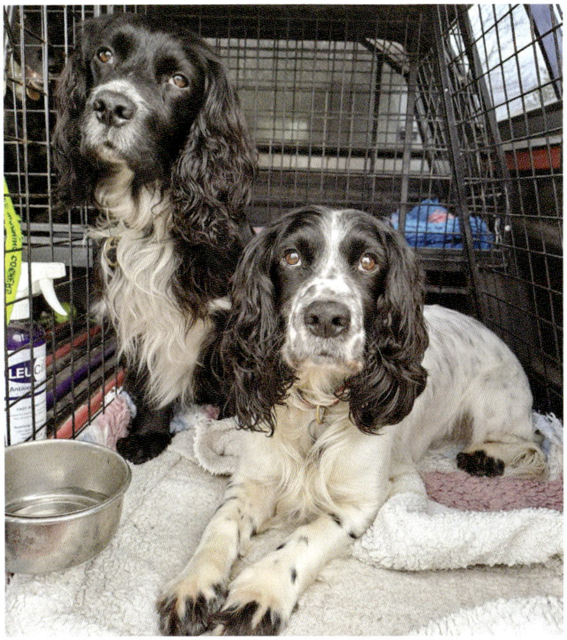

Relaxed and calm behaviour in car crates is an important skill.

What gets rewarded and rewarded well, will get repeated and become habit, like control going through a gate.

Training is about creating good behavioural habits, like this calm 'settle'.

resources? Their natural desire to carry items has resulted in items being snatched away, or they have felt challenged when eating or drinking.

By thinking carefully about why a behaviour is happening, we can understand with empathy and compassion why our spaniel is doing what they are doing. For specific behaviours, keeping a record (a diary or taking videos) of what is happening and when, can identify triggers (sights, sounds, smells, etc.). This is useful in managing the behaviour and moving forwards in modifying it.

What gets rewarded, gets repeated

To modify a behaviour from undesirable to desirable, rewarding what you do want and rewarding it well is critical. What gets rewarded gets repeated. If there is good reward and reinforcement history, behaviours become habits – why do you turn up for work each day? You might love your job, but you also get paid – rewarded. Our spaniels function in the same way – pay them well for a job well done and they are likely to do it again.

This can also work in a negative way for us. The spaniel who has learned how to chase birds or wildlife will find it highly self-rewarding, often far more so than us offering a chunk of cheese. If there has been accidental rewarding for behaviours like chasing, hunting and not recalling, then we have to do much more remedial work to get a new, alternative, and behavioural habit formed instead. Training our spaniels is all about habit forming – creating good ones and breaking (or avoiding the formation of) bad ones.

Your next challenge is deciding what behaviours are acceptable and desirable to you and which ones are

Reward-based training strategies use toys, games and food rewards to promote learning.

Reward-based training results in happy, confident spaniels.

not – what works for one person will not be ideal for another. This is also why the idea of 'one size fits all' does not work in training as well as everyday management and care.

Should I punish my spaniel?

Dog training has moved significantly towards reward-based methods, rewarding dogs for behaviours we like, rather than being punitive over behaviours that we do not like or want. Reward-based methods are successful in developing solid and consistent behaviours and from an ethical and welfare perspective are viewed as good for both dog and handler.

If rewards increase the likelihood of a behaviour reoccurring, then punishment decreases it. We live in a world where punishment (or the threat of it) is everywhere. Break the speed limit and get caught, you will get a fine and points on your licence – a punishment. It might be unpalatable, but punishment works. However, using punishment as a training strategy negatively impacts on an animal's ability to learn. Stress and fear inhibit learning and if there is fear of a negative consequence, then learning is poor. Using aversive tools such as rattle cans and shock collars is also not supported by training and behaviour organisations.

In line with current knowledge and understanding, the use of reward-based training is recommended. Deliberate punishment is not ethical, humane, or a welfare-friendly way to train – we know so much more about effective, fair and kind approaches now. We appreciate that there can be serious fallout from training that is punitive and coercive. It negatively affects the relationship between you and your spaniel and in extreme cases can result in fearful, anxious and aggressive behaviours.

Recall must always be rewarded and rewarded well.

How can I reward my spaniel to reinforce the behaviours I want?

What your spaniel will find rewarding and thus reinforcing for a behaviour varies on an individual and context-specific basis. Some spaniels love toys as rewards and enjoy playing with their handler as a reward. Others are motivated by food. Some like physical touch as a reward and others will enjoy being able to sniff, hunt or retrieve as their reward.

Explore what works for your own spaniel and in what situations and circumstances. Sometimes this will also be a result of both your own and your spaniel's prior experience. In my own training I use food and toy rewards but know that in a hierarchy of reward, food wins for all my spaniels. Draw up a 'power list' of rewards and you will always know what to bring out in what situation and when it is needed. You can provide a jackpot bonus reward from the top of your reward hierarchy – you know, that time that your spaniel recalls off a hare that pops up under their nose and returns to you, no questions asked – that is when the whole squeezy cheese tube gets squeezed into their mouth!

A food pouch toy is a great way to combine food and toy rewards in training.

Food containing toys can be closed securely and only opened to release the food with the help of the handler.

Why does my spaniel hump?

Humping or mounting is an entirely natural canine behaviour. Males mounting females is an essential part of the canine reproductive process, but mounting and humping can also be seen in less amorous situations and with a range of participants (willing and unwilling!) and objects.

It can be embarrassing but they are not trying to dominate you, nor are they necessarily over-sexed. Humans, dogs and inanimate objects such as dog beds, cushions and toys can become the target for mounting and humping. 'Air humping' is sometimes seen, in which your dog takes an imaginary humping position and posture.

Humping usually occurs when your spaniel is aroused, but this does not necessarily mean sexually! I have seen puppies in the whelping box show humping behaviour, long before they have reached sexual maturity.

Excitement, stress and anxiety can result in mounting and humping behaviour. Males and females both hump and bitches often mount each other if one is in season. Humping is also a displacement behaviour and may signify that your dog is conflicted and unsure what to do. It can also be a sign of tiredness – often seen during the evening after a busy day.

When might humping be a problem and what should you do about it?

If your spaniel is consistently humping for prolonged periods or becoming excessively aroused by it, encourage them to stop and direct to an alternative but incompatible behaviour, such as a relaxed settle. If there are specific objects of desire, limit access to them. Alternatively, only permit your spaniel to hump particular items.

If other dogs are the targets, management is essential for everyone's safety. Obviously unless mating is intended, restricting access of males to potentially fertile females is important – do not always assume that caregivers of bitches are aware of their female's reproductive state either. Plenty of in-season bitches go around their daily lives in public. If you have a male dog, you must manage their behaviour (and help them learn to manage their behaviour, too) as a result. Keeping your dog on lead and rewarding them for neutral (that is, non-contact) or calm, respectful and positive interactions with others is a good strategy. If your dog has the propensity to get excited when meeting new dogs and tries to mount them, be prepared to intervene, or carefully manage greetings and contact.

While some dogs will be very tolerant of mounting behaviour, most will not be. Spayed bitches can be the least tolerant of being mounted, but ironically, are often the ones who will mount each other when they get excited or conflicted behaviourally. Remember that many caregivers will not be tolerant of your dog mounting theirs and situations can escalate quickly when dogs start posturing with each other. Sometimes other dogs have injuries or conditions such as osteoarthritis, meaning that being mounted by an unknown dog will be distressing and painful, so do not permit it.

Dogs should be calm and respectful around dogs from other households.

THE 'SELF-TIE' – WHAT MIGHT HAPPEN FROM HUMPING

In males you might find a 'self-tie' situation as a result of humping, when the bulb at the base of their penis enlarges significantly. This would normally be part of the mating process where the male and female effectively become 'locked together' for several minutes. A self-tie can be a worry for a caregiver who sees this for the very first time, especially as dog penises are usually housed in their sheath. In most cases, a self-tie resolves itself quickly. Providing your dog is not distressed, keeping them still and quiet helps. Dogs have a bone in their penis called the os penis or baculum. Should a self-tie occur, it is important to keep your dog calm because that bone can be broken. Similarly, if you have an unwanted mating, never try to separate the dog and bitch when they have tied because you can seriously injure one or both. If a self-tie is prolonged, then gently holding a cool, wet cloth to it can help the swelling decrease. Seek veterinary support if there is an injury or a prolonged self-tie.

Coping with noise and firework fears

Fireworks, and other loud, surprising noises such as bird scarers, gunshot and jet planes can cause distress and upset for our spaniels. Many animals have an instinctive fear response to unexpected, loud noises. Mostly, they will adapt and become used to them. Early puppy exposure to a range of sounds can help develop a relaxed response to unusual sights and sounds and good breeders do exactly this.

SUPPORTING THE NOISE-SENSITIVE SPANIEL

- **Plan ahead** – Exposing young puppies to a range of sights and sounds is a simple way to minimise potential noise-reactivity problems. Good breeders will do this, but for older puppies or dogs using broadcasts with 'scary sounds' and pairing them with food or other fun things helps to develop acceptance and a relaxed response through counterconditioning and desensitisation. If the behaviour is ingrained, getting a qualified behaviourist on board will help to implement a suitable training plan.
- **Get professional advice** – especially if your spaniel is showing severe fear responses. Veterinary and behavioural advice is beneficial and complements alternative strategies such as calming supplements. These products have limited supporting evidence and might work for some dogs, but specialist help is also advised. Medication might be useful (from your vet), especially if combined with a behaviour modification plan. For older dogs, or where noise reactivity is a new behaviour, also seek veterinary advice in case there is something else going on – such as hearing or cognitive deficits, or illness or injury causing pain.
- **Help them feel safe** – Historic advice was to ignore a scared dog, so you did not 'reward' the fear. We now know that fear is an emotion and cannot be reinforced in the same way as a specific behaviour can be. So, we can help a scared spaniel by providing safety and security if they are afraid. If your spaniel seeks comfort from you, provide it. Reassure them and be kind and empathetic. A covered crate, sofa-fort, or den-like area for your spaniel to feel safe in, especially during firework season, is a good idea too. Disguising external noises with the radio, television or playing repetitive, percussive sounds like drumming can help too.
- **Use food, toys, and play** – You can distract and support your worried spaniel by providing high value food or treats, toys and games. This can help to build those positive associations with the scary thing. Food enrichment toys such as licking, or snuffle mats or food activity toys and puzzle games can help prolong activity. Allowing our dogs to sniff and use their noses can relax them and help them be more optimistic.
- **Check security and identification** – If an event with noise is planned, do check garden security and your dog's identification. Dogs often go missing when scared, so limiting this potential is key and should the worst happen, if their identification and microchip information is current, they should get home quickly. If you do take a worried dog out for a toilet break during fireworks, keep them on lead to avoid the risk of them running off.

A sofa-fort can help noise-phobic spaniels feel safe and secure.

You can also train your spaniel that certain noises predict nice things – food or a toy. For working spaniels, gunshot is directly linked to hunting and/or retrieving, which is highly rewarding, but do not assume that all spaniels will have this as an 'inbuilt' ability. Just because your spaniel is happy with gunshot, they can worry about other noises. I have one cocker who is a bulldozer of a working gundog and does not flinch on hearing gunshot, but fireworks and even car doors slamming upset her terribly.

Sometimes, dogs can develop more deep-seated distress responses to specific sounds, often linked to pain. If your spaniel has suddenly started responding negatively to noises, get them checked for potential pain by your vet. Once pain has been managed or ruled out, then you can implement measures to support your spaniel.

When can I stop training or going to classes?

Dog trainers often report fully booked puppy classes, but the attrition rate of puppies continuing to adolescent and adult classes is high. Sometimes, caregivers feel that their dog has acquired the essential skills and behaviours they need and want and off they go. For others, life gets in the way – work, children and other expectations, making attendance difficult. Sometimes the novelty and excitement of a new puppy wanes, and enthusiasm dwindles as things become challenging. There is also sometimes the idea that a series of training classes will 'program' your dog to meet a series of expectations of what a good dog should be. The reality is obviously different.

'Training is for life, not just for puppy class.'

In much the same way that we all have to constantly upskill/reskill and demonstrate forms of continuing professional and educational development in our work lives, our spaniels also benefit from the same approach. This might mean continuing to attend regular training classes and workshops or you might be

Training is for life, not just puppy class!

confident to keep honing the skills you already have, at home and when out and about.

Technology now means that you can even 'attend' classes, workshops and seminars online and there are many excellent canine coaches and trainers who make exercises and ideas freely available via social media (although do ensure that the training methods and exercises demonstrated are safe and appropriate).

Dog training is about habits. Practise and proof the good habits (and reward them well) and you can make training a way of life.

When can I stop using rewards?

'I don't want to carry treats with me for the rest of my life.'

There is definitely a real desire by many caregivers to fade out treat use as quickly as possible. The problem is that as soon as rewards become less frequent and then non-existent, behaviours we were rewarding slip in quality, quantity, and speed of performance. If your salary became intermittent, you too would be less productive and effective at work.

There is a point in reward-based training where a 'variable schedule' of reinforcement becomes powerful. This means that instead of rewarding every single 'sit' for example, you ask for a 'sit,' release your

Practise skills such as 'wait' every day with your spaniel, to make them become good habits.

dog, ask again, release your dog, then ask again and reward on this third one. Then you might ask again and reward at that point. You mix up how frequently the reward is given. This should only be started when a behaviour is robust and consistent, because otherwise you might find it becomes sloppy and your spaniel gets confused. However, what this process does start to produce is a dog who can perform chains of individual behaviours without reward after reward after reward.

Over time, you will find that reward use (whether food, toy, verbal, or physical praise) can often be reduced. I always carry some treats with me, in the same way as I always carry poo bags, but on many walks, treat use is minimal. However, when something happens that deserves a huge acknowledgement and reward, I can do that – the recall from deer, for example. Pots of treats are also strategically placed around the house, so that I can reward excellent behaviour at key places – the front door is where I want to be able to reward calmness and politeness if there is someone at the door.

Even if you are reducing the general frequency of food rewards, do not forget to ramp it up sometimes and if a behaviour is needing 'tidying up', increase the reward frequency again. Use jackpot rewards too – when your spaniel does something BRILLIANT, pull out the brilliant reward – cooked meats, cheese, cooked liver – whatever your dog covets.

Will my spaniel ever calm down?

Spaniels are busy, active dogs. If you hope for a dog who would need minimal exercise, attention or human input, a spaniel is not the best choice. However, 'calmness' is relative. I know many people who live with other breeds and types who are even busier than spaniels. It is also possible to help your spaniel learn when busyness is appropriate and when relaxing and chilling is the suitable choice.

Most spaniels learn boundaries very quickly, especially if their other needs are met. If you expect a quick five-minute, on-lead walk to tire out a spaniel, physically or mentally, you will be mistaken. Instead, you will end up with one desperate for attention, connection and something to do. If you provide an outlet for that physical and mental busyness, your spaniel will quickly learn to self-settle and regulate themselves. You might need to provide some support to help them learn this, through crate or 'settle' training, but you can absolutely have a calm spaniel at home.

When out and about, when calmness is needed, you can help your spaniel learn impulse control and self-management – effectively that they cannot always get what they want. This builds tolerance and resilience to frustration and further aids calm behaviour, but does need training, practice and proofing in lots of different places.

However, one of the joys of spaniels is that they often remain active and outgoing even into their later years. Yes, they mature and become calmer and more

Many spaniels love a ball as a high value reward.

Spaniels are naturally busy but can relax too – even in odd places!

relaxed in many situations, but they rarely lose that buzz and spark that makes them exactly who they are.

Why does my spaniel eat poo?

Eating poo (coprophagy) is a natural behaviour for the domestic dog and reflects their evolutionary origin as a successful scavenger. Dogs might eat their own faecal matter, that of other dogs, or poo from other species. It is not always a sign of a poor diet or a deficiency and just seems to be something 'that some dogs do'. Sometimes it is a learned behaviour from puppyhood if they were raised in poor conditions. Some dogs do it in anticipation of a negative response from their caregiver if poo is present. Sometimes, dogs enjoy eating poo and actively seek it out, however distasteful it is for us.

If you have a coprophagic spaniel, rule out any veterinary reasons. Limit access to poo by removing it frequently, especially if it is their own or other dogs' that is being eaten. This is far more effective than some of the many 'cures' that are not validated or effective.

Eating poo might indicate that your spaniel's gut microbiome might need some help. This population of microbes is found mostly in the small and large intestines and helps with digestive processes but is also linked to behaviour and overall wellbeing. Sometimes the health of the microbiome is not great, and it needs some help.

Feeding probiotics (live organisms fed to our dogs) and prebiotics (fibrous food in our dogs' food that effectively feeds the microbiome) can help. Faecal transfers from dogs with 'healthy' microbiomes are also beneficial. Perhaps some coprophagic dogs are undertaking their own transfer of potentially beneficial micro-organisms and this remains an area of active scientific research.

Why does my spaniel get the 'squits' during exercise?

A common complaint is the 'spaniel squits', in which the first poo on a walk or during activity is solid and as expected, but subsequent poos become less and less solid. Ruling out potential veterinary reasons for this is essential, but often it is a result of food being present in the digestive system while your spaniel is active. With physical activity, the digestive system moves and can accelerate the passage of material through it.

This is a common occurrence in long-distance (human) runners too and both the timing of eating and what is eaten can have a significant impact on its occurrence. This increased movement of the digestive system can limit the digestive process and also inhibits the normal reabsorption of water from digested material in the large intestine. As a result, this material is not fully digestively processed, and faeces are not properly formed.

If the 'squits' are an issue – important if you are competing for example – then assessing what you feed (look for highly digestible), how much you feed (smaller meals will be processed more quickly), and when you feed (leave at least an hour between feeding and exercise – the longer the better – rest and digest is an excellent mantra) is a good idea.

My spaniel often wakes early and is sick – why?

'Hunger pukes' are surprisingly common in adolescent spaniels. This is characterised by early morning waking and being sick, bringing up small amounts of frothy, creamy fluid. Do rule out veterinary causes, but in most cases, 'hunger pukes' are linked to your spaniel's digestive system 'waking up' in anticipation of breakfast and this causes sickness. Because there is no digesta in the stomach, there is nothing substantial to bring up.

Often dogs grow out of it – I have typically seen it in adolescent males from around six months to about a year old, but it does sometimes persist. Management usually involves looking at their diet and ensuring that there is enough bulk to ensure satiety. You can also feed a small meal last thing at night so that there is something in their digestive system overnight or wake earlier than they do to provide an early breakfast.

My spaniel gets very dramatic about pooping!

I am sure 'dramatic pooping' is seen in many dogs, but I routinely see it in spaniels, and it is something that has come up in many discussions in spaniel training classes. 'Dramatic pooping' refers to overly intense and dramatic behaviours immediately before defecating. In some cases, people have reported thinking their spaniel was ill, or in pain before they realised the pattern.

Allow a period of 'rest and digest' after feeding your spaniel to minimise digestive issues.

'Dramatic pooping' usually manifests as being unable to focus or respond to cues. It might mean there is frantic pulling, sniffing, circling and pacing until they eventually squat. There might also be a delay to actually pooping – almost ensuring they are pooping in 'the most perfect place' (even although you will be picking it up anyway!).

If you are concerned or it becomes prolonged or problematic, get a vet check to rule out potential digestive issues, but usually, just know it happens. If you need your spaniel to be fully 'in the room with you', making sure they have pooped beforehand, is a good idea.

My spaniel scoots their bottom along the ground – why?

If your spaniel 'scoots' their bottom along the ground, especially after pooping, they may have anal gland issues. The anal glands are located just inside the anus and sometimes do not empty naturally. This can result in discomfort and irritation. Sometimes they can become impacted and then infected. Affected dogs often chew the base of their tail or drag their bottom on the ground to relieve their discomfort. You might smell a fishy odour coming from the anal gland secretions. Sometimes anal gland problems are a result of conformation and help is needed to manually empty them.

Diet can also be a factor, especially if it produces very soft faeces that do not help the anal glands to empty naturally. Simple, helpful dietary changes include increasing the amount of fibre in the diet or adding pro- and prebiotics. These can help improve faecal bulk and consistency to support normal anal gland emptying.

Why does my spaniel eat grass and plant matter?

While much plant material is not easily digested by our dogs, they do often self-select plants and plant matter, including grass, fruit and vegetables. Consuming grass used to be thought of as a sign of illness, and dogs will sometimes eat grass as an emetic – a way of inducing sickness – but many dogs eat grass and other plants when they are quite well. Dogs also have sweet-taste receptors, explaining why they seem to enjoy and actively select young, sweet plants and many fruits. If your spaniel eats grass or other plants and are well, do not worry. Do monitor how much they eat, however, because it will not be digested, and excess amounts could create a blockage.

Plant eating is a normal behaviour enjoyed by many dogs – these spaniels are picking blackberries straight off the plant.

My spaniel is a little 'rounder' than ideal – overweight and obesity

Despite being naturally active and outgoing, many spaniels have a propensity to be 'thrifty' and gain weight. This is common in mature, adult dogs and if they have been spayed or neutered, they might be more likely to gain weight too.

Excess bodyweight is not healthy for our spaniels, affecting overall health and wellbeing, as well as reducing their lifespan. One thing we can do to help our dogs live as long and as healthy lives possible is to keep them at a healthy, lean bodyweight.

Being overweight and obesity are the most common causes of malnutrition seen in dogs. A major risk factor in the development of being overweight and obesity is the consumption of excess energy. Many dog treats and foods are highly palatable and energy (kilocalorie) dense, meaning it is easy to accidentally overfeed energy, which gets converted to stored fat in the body. Combine this with limited amounts or intensity of activity and your spaniel might gain weight.

Weight reduction and management need to consider diet and exercise. Other lifestyle factors might also be important too. Some health conditions might be linked with weight gain and living in centrally heated houses means our spaniels do not expend energy, keeping themselves warm in the same way as kennelled spaniels might.

For weight loss, a kilocalorie deficit is needed. Selecting a food with a low energy density and lower levels of fat than standard dog diets is a good strategy. Weight management foods are formulated to ensure that your spaniel is satisfied by the amount fed, but they also get the nutrients needed without excess energy.

Increase the intensity, frequency and duration of activity to increase your spaniel's metabolism and to 'burn fat.' Start sensibly and sustainably – increase their active time by a few minutes per week. Perhaps walk faster and give both you and your dog targets to meet which can also help you see progress. You could even explore a new activity for your spaniel.

Regularly weigh and body-condition score your spaniel, feeling for anatomical and body landmarks. Compare your spaniel to scoring charts to help identify if they are a healthy weight, underweight or overweight. By measuring and monitoring your spaniel's bodyweight and overall condition, you can identify subtle weight gain (or loss) before it reaches a point where serious action is needed. You should see a clear waistline when looking at your spaniel from above, an upwards abdominal tuck when viewed from the side,

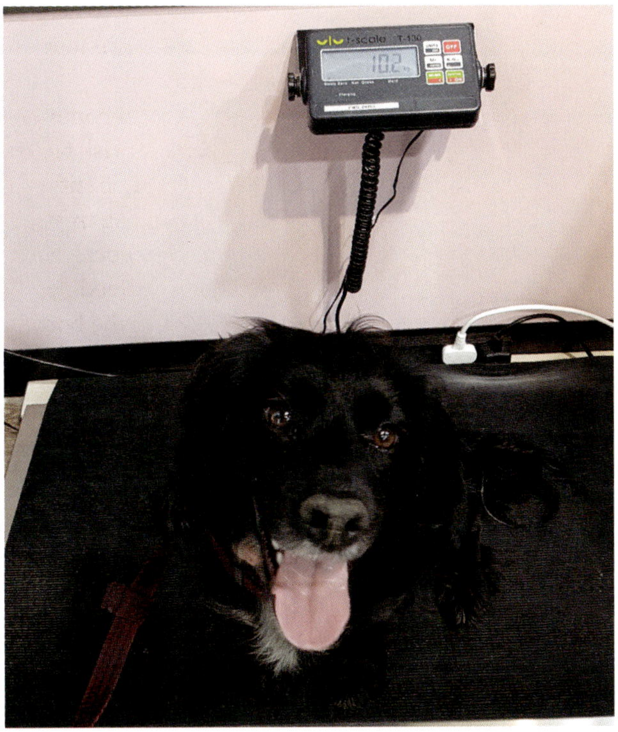

Regular weighing and body condition scoring alongside managing diet and exercise can help to keep your spaniel at a suitable, healthy weight.

and you should be able to easily feel their ribs – being able to see their ribs when they are moving is also an indication of healthy bodyweight.

Weigh their food as well, so that you know exactly how much is being fed. Do this for every meal to maintain a consistent intake of a known amount of food. If you use a scoop, only use it to weigh out food – using scoops to measure how much is being fed is notoriously inaccurate and can result in significantly more food being fed than is ideal.

Be aware of other treats, snacks and chews, and access (intended or accidental) to foods from other animals or people in the household. Consider using lower energy and healthier options such as carrot or cucumber, which are usually well accepted by dogs and make great weight management treats.

WHEN IS PROFESSIONAL INPUT NEEDED?

Social media and the internet mean that there is a wealth of information available at our fingertips, but the information quality is highly variable. Occasionally, it is dangerous and inaccurate, or at its most innocuous, lacks the nuance and detail needed for individual situations and circumstances.

Many spaniel caregivers will head to the internet as a first port of call with questions or queries relating to health, behaviour or training. The problem with this is that you have no real awareness of the legitimacy, experience, or even professional expertise and accreditations of those then giving you advice. Much advice in forums, groups or discussion pages will be based on personal experience and can be heavily biased. Sometimes the advice given is completely inappropriate, such as advising administering human medication to dogs or providing other health, nutrition and management advice, outside normal and legitimate veterinary and professional protocols. Such advice typically comes without formal back up, support, client protection or insurance.

Similarly, for behaviour and training advice, the internet can be a trickly place to assess what is good, effective and 'best practice.' If someone answers a question with absolutes – 'do this' – without asking further questions, then that is a major red flag. There is nuance about our dogs, and they are individuals. Their situations and circumstances are unique. One size does not fit all and to assume otherwise is a significant failing.

Good professional advice will consider nuance and will rarely provide definitive answers without more detail. This is important to consider all potentials and also to identify what will work best for individual dog and caregiver. If someone says, 'it depends,' then view that as a sign that you will likely get competent and accurate support and advice. Equally, while it might be tempting to save money by seeking advice for free, remember that professionals have spent time and money honing their experience, knowledge and skills. Circumventing this might actually cost you more overall (as well as being potentially harmful for your dog), so seeking suitably qualified persons to support you is essential.

When seeking professional help, look for credentials and qualifications. Professional memberships can also be a good sign that someone is investing in continued education, professional development and will be compliant with codes of conduct and ethics. Just because someone has had spaniels for years, does not mean that they are as experienced or as current in their knowledge as you might think.

Love, cherish and enjoy your spaniel.

WHEN TO SEEK PROFESSIONAL INPUT?

Knowing when to seek external advice and support is not always obvious, but here are some situations when professional input is strongly recommended.

- Acute and painful health conditions such as injury, lethargy, obvious and significant lameness, prolonged digestive upset (longer than a few hours with no resolution), extreme diarrhoea/vomiting (especially in very young or older dogs), movement or performance changes and any new lumps/bumps.
- Any unusual and sustained behavioural change such as aggression (to people, dogs or other animals), lethargy or unusual noise reactivity.
- If you have become 'stuck' on a specific aspect of training, such as recall or skills for a particular discipline or activity.

In most cases, your vet is a great first port of call and can often direct you to other canine professionals who might be well placed to help too.

TOP TIPS FOR SURVIVING YOUR SPANIEL

- In the event of concerning behavioural or health issues, ***always*** seek appropriately qualified and professional advice from your veterinary surgeon, behaviourist or other canine professional – social media is not best placed to support or advise you.
- A spaniel-savvy trainer can be a huge support to you, giving you advice, guidance and even training tips and exercises that tap into the spaniel mindset.
- Remember what your spaniel's ancestors were bred to do – this can help us understand and work WITH them and their inbuilt drives and characteristics, rather than trying to suppress them.
- Your sense of humour is essential – if you can smile and laugh when it is all going a bit wrong, then you will be fine, and your spaniel will be all the happier for having a relaxed handler.
- Try not to take things too seriously – tomorrow is always another day to work, train or compete and your spaniel may well not be taking things too seriously either!
- Know that having matching socks, shoes, personal space and not having to remove a spaniel from your spot on the sofa are potentially things of the past.
- Smile, relax and enjoy your spaniel and the time you get to spend together – it is a sad reality that they simply are not around as long as we would like them to be.
- Remember, training is all about forming good habits (behaviours) and minimising the formation of poor ones.
- Reward and reinforce your spaniel generously for desired behaviour – what gets rewarded, gets repeated.
- Limit and manage your spaniel's ability to rehearse unwanted or undesirable behaviours – rehearsal will only mean they get better at them.
- Be prepared for a potential spaniel addiction – many people report the phenomenon of 'not being able to have just one!'.
- Treasure them – they are not around as long as we would like them to be – even when you are rolling your eyes at their antics, know that one day, those antics will only be memories.

FURTHER READING

Arden, J., *Mission Control: How to train the high-drive dog* (First Stone Publishing, UK, 2020)

Boyd, J., *Canine Nutrition. Food, feeding and Function* (The Crowood Press, UK, 2023)

Case, L., *The Dog – Its Behaviour, Nutrition and Health* (3rd edition, Wiley-Blackwell, UK, 2023)

Krauss, K. and Maue, G., *Dogs in Translation* (First Stone Publishing, UK, 2022)

McDevitt, L., *Control Unleashed* (Clean Run Productions, LLC, UK, 2015)

Mueller, S., *Hunting Together – Harnessing Predatory Chasing in Family Dogs Through Motivation-Based Training* (2nd edition, Predation Substitute Training, UK, 2023)

Mueller, S., *Walking Together – Loose Lead Walking for High Energy Dogs* (Predation Substitute Training, UK, 2024)

Zulch, H. and Mills, D., *Life Skills for Puppies* (Hubble and Hattie, UK, 2012)

INDEX

First published in 2025 by
The Crowood Press Ltd
Ramsbury, Marlborough
Wiltshire SN8 2HR

enquiries@crowood.com
www.crowood.com

British Library Cataloguing-in-Publication Data
A catalogue record for this book is available from the British Library.

For product safety-related questions contact productsafety@crowood.com.

ISBN 978 0 7198 4502 4

The right of Jacqueline Boyd to be identified as author of this work has been asserted by her in accordance with the Copyright, Designs and Patents Act 1988.

Typeset by Simon & Sons
Cover design by Su Richards
Printed and bound in India by Nutech Print Services

Acknowledgements

Huge thanks to my fabulous family and friends, who have offered supportive and nagging words of wisdom during the writing, editing and thinking about this book.

To everyone who provided lovely spaniel photos – thank you! I hope you enjoy seeing some of them in print.

To the team at Crowood – you are wonderful – thank you again.

Finally, this is for Megan, Brantz, Molly, Bobbi, Austin, Mini-Moo, Bertie, Pixie and Mirabelle Moon and all the other Clonameg Cockers – you all make me want to be a better person and make the world a better place for dogs.

Photo acknowledgements

Photographs are by the author except for the following: sincere thanks are extended to Kenny Drew of EventFaces Photography: pp 100, 123; Sarah and Lucy Heckford: pp 13, 39, 45; Louise Scott: pp 10, 28, 114, 118, 119, 124, 151; Kirsty Mitchell: pp 21, 27, 85; Alex Porter: pp 31, 38, 41, 102, 107, 109, 139, 143, 146, 152, 153; Emily Birch: pp 11, 14, 26, 42; Rebecca Harding: pp 22, 69, 116; Kate Horton: pp 32, 55, 71, 141; Hannah Thompson: pp 42, 137; Fraser Boyd: p. 72; Emily Watterson: p. 4.

Cover photograph by Kenny Drew of EventFaces Photography (eventfaces.co.uk). Back cover photographs by the author (left and right) and Kenny Drew of EventFaces Photography (centre).